Simple and Quick
DIET
COOKBOOK:
How to Lose Weight and Stay Healthy

BY
Hannelore Blohm
AND
Dr. H. D. Cremer

BARRON'S

Woodbury, New York • London • Toronto • Sydney

Credits
Color photos are from Teubner-Studio,
    Fussen Grofe und Unzer GmbH.
Translation: Helen Feingold
Americanization and Adaptation: Patricia Connell

First English language edition published in 1985 by Barron's Educational Series, Inc.

Originally published in German under the title
Abnehmen-Einfach, Schnell, Gesund
© 1979 by Grafe und Unzer GmbH, Munchen, West
    Germany

All inquiries should be addressed to:
Barron's Educational Series, Inc.
113 Crossways Park Drive
Woodbury, New York 11797

International Standard Book No. 0-8120-5659-0

Library of Congress Catalog Card No. 84-24494

Library of Congress Cataloging in Publication Data

Blohm, Hannelore.
  The simple and quick diet book

  Translation of: Abnehmen — einfach, schnell, gesund.
  Includes index.
  1. Low-calorie diet — Recipes. I. Cremer, H.-D.
(Hans-Diedrich), 1910-   . II. Title.
RM222.2.B68513   1985   613.2'5   84-24494
ISBN 0-8120-5659-0

PRINTED IN JAPAN

5678 230 98765432

Contents

Preface
by Dr. Hans-Diedrich Cremer

Correct, high-quality nutrition is the foundation for health, well-being and peak performance. Sorry to say, many people are not eating correctly due to ignorance, lack of willpower or indifference. The outcome of poor nutrition is nutrition deficiency, which is found in every country on earth. Here in the West, the chief nutritional error is overeating, which results in diabetes, heart disease and circulatory problems.

Overweight people know the consequences of added weight, since they invariably feel better when they slim down. For most, however, losing weight is very difficult. This handy book, full of practical advice, will help. It presents a varied diet of healthy, tasty, low-calorie dishes that will help you reduce in your own way. By and large, these foods can be cooked for the entire family; only the overweight members must adhere closely to the prescribed amounts.

For those who wish to lose a few pounds quickly there are rules for low-calorie days on weekends. Fifteen special diets are listed here: for example, an apple diet, a rice diet and a sauerkraut diet. These regimens are nutritionally one-sided and should not be followed for too long. But they are appropriate for weekend dieters who want their belts tighter, and most of these diets cater to specific tastes.

Also included is information about the nutritional and caloric value of each recipe. This will be useful not only for those who are overweight but for all who want a well-balanced diet.

Introduction
by Hannelore Blohm

The Venus di Milo, one of the most renowned sculptures of ancient Greece, can be seen today in the Louvre. If she lived nowadays she would wear a size 18, if not 20.

But her Junoesque roundness would not be our ideal of beauty. If only all the size 18s and 20s had lived in ancient Greece! But today every third person in the United States is as overweight as the Venus di Milo. Nearly every seventh youngster is too fat. Of course, vanity plays a large part in wishing to lose that weight. But when waistbands start to pinch discomfort sets in, and with many pounds one fears that the excess cannot be controlled. Overweight brings multiple health problems. It can lead to diabetes, arthritis, gout, arteriosclerosis, gallstones, liver disease and many other maladies that can be prevented by a sensible, knowledgeable diet.

I would like to help you to begin the battle against your extra pounds. Years ago, at 5'6" and weighing 165 pounds, I began to eat less food—low in sugar and fat, but rich in protein—divided into five meals daily. I know how difficult it is to see even a two-pound loss on the scale, and it took six months to lose 37 pounds. It was really never easy. But I learned what to eat and altered my eating habits, and that was the major step in becoming slimmer. I will note all my discoveries and urge you not to be discouraged when the pointer on the scale stops moving down—at the beginning the pounds are lost quickly, especially by those who are very overweight.

I also know how important it is to eat tasty and, above all, satisfying dishes while dieting. You will see that slimming foods can be delicious. With the recipes that I recommend, you will nourish your body correctly with a healthy, varied diet. You can follow this diet for as long as you wish.

In these 104 pages you will find delicious, slimming recipes with colorful photos that I hope will inspire you to start your diet today. If you stay on this path, it will lead with certainty to your ideal weight—and with the help of the recipes you can stay thin forever.

I wish you much success!

Read Before Beginning

To eat well and still become (or stay) slim is a serious problem for many. But you will lose steadily with the help of these tips and recipes. Always remember that if you want to reduce you must feel satisfied while cutting down on fat and refined carbohydrates. The ground rules for accomplishing this are:

1. Sharply reduce the proportion of fats in your food.
2. Reduce sugar by using non-caloric sweeteners.
3. Take the necessary carbohydrates in the form of fruit and vegetables.
4. Increase the amount of protein foods, as these are filling and satisfying.
5. Instead of "three squares," eat five small meals without increasing the total calorie count.
6. Drink no alcohol, but use low-calorie sweeteners if desired.

This book's practical medically proven advice is built on these basic rules. You will be surprised at how delicious the food is and at the generous size of the portions.

This program is built on a daily count of 1500 calories. Breakfast is fixed at about 375 calories, and morning and afternoon snacks at 150 calories each. This leaves 825 calories to be divided however you like between lunch, dinner and optional 100-calorie snacks. As you will see when you get to the recipes, there is a broad range of calorie counts for lunch and dinner to allow the greatest flexibility in your diet: some days you may want to divide the count fairly evenly, while at other times it will be more convenient to have a lighter midday meal and heartier dinner, or vice-versa. The choice will very likely depend on whether you have lunch at home or prepare it ahead to eat at work.

If you have soup before a meal, or want dessert afterward, you must figure in that dish and eliminate those calories elsewhere. If you'd like to lose weight faster by consuming even fewer calories, omit "accompaniment" foods or between-meal snacks.

All the recipe ingredients are chosen for nutritional balance. No matter which recipes you choose, the resulting diet will contain the right amounts of protein, fat, and carbohydrates for daily requirements. Exact food values are stated for each recipe.

The program is adaptable to home and work. In the chapter on "Take-to-Work Meals" you will find recipes and tips for dieting on the job.

Do You Know How Many Calories You Need?

The first step is calculating your ideal weight. Here is a simple formula:

Women: Allow 100 pounds for your first 5 feet of height. For each inch over 5 feet, add 5 pounds; for each inch under, subtract 5 pounds.

Example:
for 5'4"   100 pounds (for first 5 feet)
       + 20 pounds (for additional 4 inches)
        120 pounds

Men: Allow 105 pounds for your first 5 feet of height. For each inch over 5 feet, add 6 pounds; for each inch under, subtract 6 pounds.

Example:
for 5'10"   105 pounds (for first 5 feet)
       + 60 pounds (for additional 10 inches)
        165 pounds

For either sex, subtract 10 percent if you are particularly small-boned; add 10 percent if you are large-boned.

To estimate your calorie needs according to your weight and activity level, use this chart; simply multiply your present weight by the number which corresponds to your sex and activity classification. (Note that "very active" means just that—if you are not a lumberjack, gymnast or the like, don't cheat by including yourself in this category!)

ACTIVITY LEVEL	MEN	WOMEN
Sedentary	16	14
Moderately active	21	18
Very active	26	22

Example: if you are a 125-pound sedentary woman (say, an office worker who does not follow a regular exercise program), you will maintain your present weight if you consume 14 × 125, or 1750, calories daily. If you reduce to 110 pounds and want to maintain that weight without increasing your activity level, you will have to limit your daily intake to 1540 calories.

About Calories

You know already, of course, that the calorie is the unit of measurement for our energy needs and the energy supplied by our food. One gram of protein averages 4.1 calories, 1 gram of carbohydrate 4.1 calories, 1 gram of fat 9.3 calories, and 1 gram of alcohol 7.1 calories. Each recipe includes a mention of its calorie count.

Importance of Nutrition for Basic Needs and Work Needs

The body has different calorie requirements when at work and at rest. The *basic needs* are the calories required when the body is resting (for example, during sleeping or sunbathing), and thus functioning at normal temperature. The general rule is that 1 calorie is required per kilogram (2.2 pounds) of body weight for each hour at rest. Without additional exercise, you will lose 2.2 pounds per week by consuming 1000 fewer calories each day.

In Three Months, 26 Pounds Lighter

Check the table beginning on page 109 to see how many calories you have been taking daily; you will surely be surprised at how far you have surpassed your quota. If you hold fast to the rule of 1000 calories less—or to 1500 calories daily—you can, with the help of these recipes, lose 26 pounds in three months.

Exercise Makes You Feel Good!

Many believe that weight loss will occur with exercise alone. This is only possible if increased energy needs do not lead to the consumption of more calories.

Here are a few examples of the calories consumed in 30 minutes of activity:

Cooking	48 calories
Walking	51
Cleaning	57
Polishing shoes	63
Washing dishes	76
Painting	88 calories
Shopping	90
Ironing	91
Making beds	91
Driving	96
Weeding	133
Dancing	171
Sawing	185
Playing tennis	225
Playing football	232
Bicycling	234
Climbing stairs	249
Shoveling snow	250
Running	386

Please consider how long you iron or shovel snow! The largest calorie expenditure occurs when running. But no matter how much you exercise, to lose weight you cannot eat more calories than you use in a day.

Stress Creates Cravings

A knowledge not only of nutrition but also of psychology is needed to find out just why every third person is overweight, and why many overeat. Normally, each person has his own satisfaction level: at the beginning of a meal he eats faster, then more slowly, until he is full. Students of nutrition have found, however, that people under stress eat more than usual. Overweight people are the most susceptible: when they are stressed, their appetite is larger, with a higher-than-normal satisfaction level. In the course of a meal they eat too quickly and too much, and are never satisfied. Researchers have not yet found what causes the feeling of satisfaction. They only know that psychological factors play as important a role as the food itself.

Psychologists recommend the following tricks for keeping your food intake under control:

- Eat and drink slowly. The satisfaction level is reached after 15 to 20 minutes, but you can eat a great deal past this level if you eat too quickly.
- Enjoy chewing and savoring every morsel. After each bite place the silverware on the plate; after every swallow place the glass on the table. In this way it is not hard to maintain control until satisfaction is reached. With thoughtful eating, one listens to one's body and maintains control.
- Do not make meals a great occasion, as overweight families often do. Mealtime should be satisfying, but casual—not of major importance.

3

- Monitor your weight. Keep a record of every pound lost. It will spur you on to further results.
- Stretch your body's endurance with walking and stair climbing. This will improve circulation and general body tone, and you will benefit by becoming lighter on your feet.

- Join a group of other people who are reducing. Each will help the others to persevere.
- Never shop when you are hungry. It leads to overbuying and higher consumption.
- And don't forget to tell everyone that you are losing weight. This will strengthen your determination and keep you from weakening.

4

The Wrong Excuses and Reducing Fads

When I was fat I was convinced that there were good reasons for it—after all, grandma is as big and fat as I am, so I must have the same build. Fat people love to make up excuses for not losing weight. Many are very convincing. For example:

1. *Excuse:* My bones are large. A human skeleton does not weigh more than 22 pounds and does not determine the size of the body. Overweight stems primarily from fat masses.

2. *Excuse:* I became fat when I stopped smoking. Error: One does not just become fatter when smoking stops. Weight gain results when cigarettes are eliminated and candy, snacks and more food are substituted.

3. *Excuse:* I am such a good eater that I cannot reduce. Error: Your mother, out of misdirected love, made you into a good eater. She probably overfed you as a baby. It increased the quantity and size of your fat cells and helped you to achieve today's fat deposits. When you reduce, the number of fat cells remains constant but the amount of fat per cell changes and the cells shrink.

And here are some popular reducing fads:

1. Lemonade or diluted vinegar makes you thin. *False:* There is nothing wrong with a glass of lemonade (sweetened with non-caloric sweetener) or a glass of watered vinegar between meals. They can diminish your appetite, but they do not make you thin. And lemon juice has calories.

2. If I put less in my stomach, it will shrink and then I won't be able to eat so much. *False:* The stomach does not shrink. But as you learn to eat correctly, your appetite gets smaller.

3. You can lose weight in a sauna. *False:* What you lose in a sauna is two to three quarts of water, which are quickly regained when you drink. However, the sauna is beneficial in that it improves circulation and hastens removal of body wastes.

4. You can lose pounds with the use of laxatives. *False:* Laxatives do not reduce fat, but they do disturb proper digestion. And when you have digestive problems, you should quickly return to a balanced diet and correct them with the addition of natural bulk such as wheat bran.

Appetite Stoppers— a Short List

Whatever food or drink satisfies and still makes you thin is praiseworthy indeed. When you run around with a constantly grumbling stomach you become annoyed, tired and quick to give up a well-intended reducing diet. This won't happen if you pick up five meals a day from the recipe suggestions in this book.

But during the first eight or 10 days of a reducing diet you may have great cravings for your favorite foods. You believe that you cannot do without a steak and fries or a hot fudge sundae, and you think that just one time won't hurt. Stop! It's time for a warning: If you give up now, you will try again and again and never reduce.

It is hard when the first euphoric days of substantial weight loss are over, particularly for those who are very overweight. The day will come when only a small amount of weight is lost in what seems a long period of time. But don't get discouraged. Above all, do not go back to your old eating habits. If you stick with the diet, your new habits will be with you always. And so that you will not go back and feed your fat pockets, here are a few appetite stoppers to help you in the battle against cravings:

• *Two glasses of water.* As soon as you have the urge to eat or prepare a high-calorie meal, quickly drink two glasses of plain or mineral water one right after the other. Go for a walk or engage in some other activity to forget your stomach.

• *Cucumber.* Make sure you always have raw vegetables in the house—cucumbers, carrots, radishes, celery. When you feel hungry, eat as much as you want. Your stomach will be satisfied, and the vitamins, minerals and fiber are good for you.

• *Hot broths.* These work wonders. Dissolve 1 teaspoon instant broth in hot water and savor the bouillon in small sips.

• *The handwork trick.* Handwork, embroidery, knitting or crocheting is for many women a good substitute for snacking. In working to finish the project, you forget your appetite—the project becomes more important than the eating.

• *Sour satisfies.* If you crave something sour, you can eat mustard and dill pickles, cornichons and sour (but not sweet-sour) pickle slices as much as you want. Or have sauerkraut as a snack. The calorie count is so small as to be insignificant.

• *Sports and sleep.* Sports distract you from eating and make you tired; earlier sleep keeps you from eating to excess. But don't turn in with a grumbling stomach. Have an appetite stopper before you go to bed.

Correct Amounts, Correct Eating

A normal kitchen scale is not exact enough for many of the small measurements in these recipes. Your reducing diet's success depends on these precise measurements to teach you to eat correctly; it cannot be done by eye, as this is misleading. Can you tell how much 1 teaspoon of butter is just by eyeballing it? Or when a slice of cheese or bread weighs 1 ounce? No; exact measurements must be made at the beginning, until you are certain of your portions. In many cases measuring spoons and cups are suitable for accurate measurement, but the only way to be sure of the proper amounts of bread, meat, cheese and so on is with a good kitchen scale. If you are not sure of the capacity of a measuring spoon, its contents can be weighed exactly on a postage scale. Note that bread slices are different weights depending on the recipe, and it is important that you adhere closely to the measurements. For example, $\frac{1}{2}$ ounce of wheat bread contains 24 calories; slices weighing $\frac{1}{2}$ ounce too much raise your calorie count without your realizing it.

When you weigh bread, butter and cheese a few times, you will get a feel for the correct weight of these and other foods. But please follow the measurements in the recipes, so not an extra ounce stands in the way of your weight loss.

It is not necessary to be so exact when measuring herbs. A tablespoon of chives, for example, weighs very little and is very low in calories, so a little more will not hurt ($3\frac{1}{2}$ ounces of herbs, much more than you would use in a recipe, contains only 46 calories).

Perhaps it will be helpful for you to remember the following volumes:

1 cup liquid is 16 tablespoons and is the capacity of a soup bowl.
$\frac{1}{2}$ cup liquid is 8 tablespoons.
$\frac{1}{4}$ cup is 4 tablespoons.
2 tablespoons liquid fill a shot glass.

Drinks Also Have Calories

Our bodies, being 60% liquid, need lots of water, which of course is calorie-free. But juices and alcoholic drinks can be laden with calories. Here's a list of their various counts.

2 tablespoons = a shot glass
4 tablespoons = a double shot glass
5 tablespoons = a wine glass

A dry wine or champagne glass holds $6\frac{1}{2}$ tablespoons. Beer glasses vary a great deal; fill yours from a measuring cup to find out its capacity.

All vegetable juices, unsweetened fruit juices, club soda and mineral water, black tea, fruit or herb teas (sweetened with low-calorie sugar substitutes) and also buttermilk are good low-calorie thirst quenchers.

	QUANTITY	CALORIES
Ale	$1\frac{1}{3}$ cups	146
Anisette	2 tablespoons	75
Apple juice	$\frac{3}{4}$ cup	94
Apple wine	1 cup	115
Apricot brandy	2 tablespoons	65
Beer, light	$1\frac{1}{3}$ cups	80
Beer, malt	$1\frac{1}{3}$ cups	185

	QUANTITY	CALORIES
Beer, pilsner	$1\frac{1}{3}$ cups	146
Beet juice	$\frac{1}{3}$ cup	32
Blackberry juice, unsweetened	$\frac{3}{4}$ cup	72
Blueberry juice, unsweetened	$\frac{3}{4}$ cup	126
Brandy	2 tablespoons	44
Calvados	2 tablespoons	65
Campari	2 tablespoons	85
Carrot juice	$\frac{3}{4}$ cup	54
Champagne, dry	$\frac{1}{3}$ cup	58
Champagne, sweet	$\frac{1}{3}$ cup	65
Cherry juice, unsweetened	$\frac{3}{4}$ cup	132
Chicory coffee	1 cup	3
Club soda		0
Cocoa	1 cup	138
Coffee		0
Eggnog	2 tablespoons	50
Espresso		0
Gin	2 tablespoons	65
Grape juice	$\frac{3}{4}$ cup	148
Grapefruit juice, unsweetened	$\frac{3}{4}$ cup	54

	QUANTITY	CALORIES
Herb liqueur	2 tablespoons	52
Herb tea		0
Kirsch	2 tablespoons	67
Madeira	$\frac{1}{3}$ cup	59
Mineral water		0
Orange juice	$\frac{1}{3}$ cup	35
Plum juice	$\frac{1}{3}$ cup	77
Prune juice	2 tablespoons	60
Rum, golden	2 tablespoons	74
Rum, white	2 tablespoons	50
Sherry, dry	$\frac{1}{3}$ cup	49
Sherry, sweet	$\frac{1}{3}$ cup	77
Slivovitz	2 tablespoons	60
Strawberry juice, unsweetened	$\frac{3}{4}$ cup	48

	QUANTITY	CALORIES
Tea		0
Tea with 1 teaspoon sugar		19
Tomato juice	$\frac{3}{4}$ cup	42
Vermouth, dry	$\frac{1}{3}$ cup	57
Vermouth, sweet	$\frac{1}{3}$ cup	85
Vodka	2 tablespoons	45
Water		0
Whiskey	$\frac{1}{4}$ cup	115
Wine, red	1 cup	175
Wine, rosé	1 cup	175
Wine, white	1 cup	182

If There Is an Overweight Child in the Family

As adults, we can determine whether we will be fat or thin. But we must also answer for our children, since they have no knowledge of nutrition and will eat what they are given.

Today nearly one of every seven American children is overweight. During the last decade the incidence of childhood obesity increased alarmingly—from 10% in 1966 to 15% in 1978. This is a 50% jump in just a dozen years.

- Almost 20% of small children have pot bellies because of high fat foods.
- Around 30% of all school children between six and eight years are ridiculed by their fellow students because they are fat and therefore clumsy and sluggish.

It is a fact that overweight children have a tougher life. Their extra pounds frequently cause poor posture and foot damage. Since fat deposits must be nourished with blood, the heart and circulation are adversely affected. With strenuous body activity heavy children are quickly out of breath, so they learn to prefer inactivity. They can become ill with such maladies as high blood pressure. Other than this, fat children suffer psychologically when they are ridiculed by their slender peers. And keep this frightening fact in mind: statistically, the odds against an overweight adolescent becoming a normal-weight adult are 28 to one.

Why are so many youngsters fat? Usually because of their parents, who lay the foundation for their children's eating habits. The following errors, for example, are widespread:

- Some anxious mothers always feed the baby when it cries. A child is not always hungry when it cries, but many mothers believe they can quiet the baby easily by feeding it.
- As with babies, small children are also pacified with food. If it is not the parents, then often grandparents or other relatives give sweets for comfort.
- Neglectful parents can create obese children, who look to food for comfort if their parents have no time for them. Child psychologists have long known that children eat or nibble as a substitute when the necessary attention is missing. This is also true for teenagers, and many of you have been making this substitution your whole lives. You seek comfort in overeating.

The parent who takes this information to heart at the beginning, when the children are small, is doing the right thing. Whoever has a chubby toddler, a plump school-age child or an overweight teenager should try psychological tricks to remove the pounds.

- Bamboozle the baby a little. Give it a bottle of anise or fennel tea, or unsweetened fruit juice, between regular feedings.
- Give a small child sweet fruit or a carrot instead of candy. Try diverting him by playing with him more often.
- If you have a school-age child who tends to be fat, don't talk constantly about the weight problem. Convince him by your example.
- Teenagers can be enthusiastic dieters but must be careful not to go too far; the risks of radical underweight and anorexia have been given much media attention in recent years.
- Please forget the saying that fat children have an extra margin. Slim children overcome illnesses better and have more joy in living.

Basic Rules for Children's Nutrition

It is even more important for children than for adults to have a high-protein diet. Children 7 to 9 years of age need 1.8 grams of protein for each 2.2 pounds of body weight; children from 10 to 14 years, 1.5 grams. At 15 to 18 years only 1.2 grams protein for each 2.2 pounds is required. Protein-rich foods include meat, poultry, fish, cheese and other milk products, and lean sausage or cold cuts; the leaner, the higher the protein content. For example, if you give your child 3½ ounces of beef, 3½ ounces of cod, and 1 cup milk in the course of a day, he will have 45 grams of protein. See pages 105 and 106 for more information on proteins.

It is very important that your child eat plenty of vegetables and fruits (but not too many bananas, as they are high in calories). These provide vitamins, minerals and other trace elements, as well as plenty of bulk for proper elimination. Whole-grain bread is also a good source of fiber. Every food that is slimming for grownups is suitable for overweight children too.

Do not listen to requests for sweets. Nothing is wrong with an *occasional* piece of chocolate, and once in a while a candy cannot hurt. But there it should stay. For everyday, offer fruit as a substitute.

Children should drink at least 2 quarts of liquid daily. Milk is good for its protein and calcium con-

tent. Freshly squeezed or unsweetened frozen fruit juices, weak tea with lemon, fruit and herb teas are all good. The older school child can drink a little diluted coffee with breakfast. But don't make the mistake of allowing children to get used to high-calorie sodas and other sweetened drinks.

Breakfast and school lunches for overweight children should limit the amount of butter or margarine served on bread. As a substitute, use low-calorie cheeses, yogurt, an egg and, with them, raw foods such as tomatoes, cucumber and radishes.

Correct Weights for Children

Please consult the chart below. The caloric requirement is figured on the base of 1000 calories. For each year are added 100 calories. Look at the chart and decide whether your child needs to lose weight.

ESTIMATED AVERAGE WEIGHTS		
Girls		
AGE	HEIGHT (INCHES)	WEIGHT (POUNDS)
3	37	31
4	40	36
5	43	40
6	45	45
7	48	50
8	50	55
9	52	61
10	55	68
11	57	77
12	60	89
13	62	100
14	64	112
15	65	120
16	65	123

Boys		
AGE	HEIGHT (INCHES)	WEIGHT (POUNDS)
3	38	32
4	41	37
5	43	40
6	46	45
7	48	50
8	50	55
9	53	60
10	55	67

AGE	HEIGHT (INCHES)	WEIGHT (POUNDS)
11	57	74
12	59	83
13	61	94
14	64	107
15	67	120
16	69	131

Here are a few precautions to take in a reducing diet for children:

1. Serve five small meals a day.

2. Give protein-rich foods.
3. Do not thicken sauces with flour. Serve low-fat salads and let the children eat as much as they want.
4. Use only lean foods.
5. Reduce the fat intake to only 2 ounces per day.
6. Lessen the consumption of (you need not completely eliminate) sugar, cake, pastries, sodas and other sweets.
7. See that the child exercises and participates in sports. The more he plays ball, rides a bicycle, or does gymnastics, the easier it is to make the diet work.

Good Recipes

Forget the myths that such foods as bread and potatoes will make you fat. It is not these foods, or recipes made with them, that are at fault. Fat comes from overeating. For example, if you eat 100 calories too much in one day, at the end of the year you will have consumed 36,500 extra calories. This is the amount of calories in 4 quarts of oil or 40 pounds of roast pork—quite a sum! No one food is to blame. The magic word is a balanced, varied diet for proper nutrition. And when it is followed during weight loss it has several good points.

Over a long period of time, a one-sided diet leads invariably to nutritional deficiencies. A satisfying, low-calorie, well-varied diet prevents deficiency, supplying everything that the body needs. Fruit, vegetables and cereals provide the necessary carbohydrates and at the same time are sources of vitamins and minerals. Proteins are in lean fish, poultry, meat and milk products. Plant oils are rich in the unsaturated fatty acids needed by the body. A varied diet supplies all the nutrients necessary to buoyant health.

This 1500-calorie-a-day program will let you lose weight normally, while keeping healthy and satisfied. The recipes in this book are not only nourishing and varied; they are also delicious, because to lose weight, a dieter must enjoy the foods permitted to him.

All of the recipes are shown in photographs that will make your mouth water. Healthy between-meal snacks are also provided to keep your stomach from growling and make it feasible to eat five meals a day. Since your stomach is never empty, hunger pangs do not occur; your appetite for your main meals is normal, not ravenous. And it has been proven in experiments that eating five meals per day, instead of the usual three, makes for the greatest chance of losing weight.

You will also find suggestions for nibbles to curb your appetite, and there are a few low-calorie sweets. You can and should eat as much as you want of plain vegetables or salad with very little oil. And remember that there is nothing wrong with eliminating a between-meal or 100-calorie snack if you wish to lose weight faster.

We have put this book together in pictures to show that it is fun to lose weight by eating sensibly and well.

Slimming Breakfasts

Sorry to say, in most families nothing is so boring, repetitious and lacking in nutrition as breakfast. It could be the good beginning of a day—but not when it consists of bread with butter and marmalade, gulped with a cup of coffee. You fast become hungry again as a high-carbohydrate meal is digested, but not when breakfast is made up of whole-grain bread, cottage cheese, yogurt, lean meats and cheese, to which are added cucumber, tomato, an egg or vegetable juice. A breakfast like this supplies all the needed nutrients: good carbohydrates, vitamins, minerals and other trace elements, with a large part of the daily requirement of protein. It gives a good start to the whole day.

Protein Breakfast

1 serving

½ cup buttermilk

Non-caloric sweetener or salt and pepper

1 tablespoon chopped chives

2 slices crispbread

1 tablespoon whipped butter or margarine

2 thin slices (1 ounce) Edam cheese

2 thin slices (½ ounce) ham

1 plum tomato, sliced

Preparation: 10 minutes

Contains 21 g protein, 33 g carbohydrate, 18 g fat

Season the buttermilk with sweetener or salt and pepper. Stir in chives or sprinkle them over the top of the buttermilk if it is not sweetened. Spread the crispbread with butter, then top one with cheese and one with ham, garnishing both with tomato slices. Sprinkle the chives on the tomatoes if you have sweetened the buttermilk.

375 calories

Grilled Toast

1 serving

1 slice toast

1 teaspoon butter

1 slice (1 ounce) boiled ham

1 slice (½ ounce) Edam cheese

1 teaspoon margarine

1 egg

Salt

1 tablespoon chopped chives

½ cup cranberry juice

Preparation: 20 minutes

Contains 17 g protein, 26 g carbohydrate, 20 g fat

Spread toast with butter. Top with ham and cheese. Broil until cheese melts. Melt margarine in small skillet. Break egg into pan; season with salt and fry. Place on toast. Sprinkle with chives. Serve with juice.

360 calories

Holiday Breakfast

1 serving

1 egg

1 teaspoon butter

Salt and sweet paprika

1 slice whole-grain rye bread

1 ounce lean liverwurst

1 slice crispbread

2 teaspoons whipped butter or margarine

1 plum tomato, sliced

1 cup tomato juice

Onion salt

Preparation: 15 minutes

Contains 12 g protein, 57 g carbohydrate, 10 g fat

Soft-cook the egg; shell and place into a small dish. Add butter, let melt and season egg with salt and

paprika. Spread the rye bread with liverwurst; spread crispbread with butter. Arrange tomato slices on bread. Serve tomato juice seasoned with onion salt.

375 calories

Chicken Sandwich

1 serving

1 cup tomato juice

Salt and white pepper

1 slice whole-grain wheat bread

1 teaspoon butter or margarine

3½ ounces cooked sliced chicken, skinned and boned

1 teaspoon catsup

Watercress

1 slice crispbread

Preparation: 10 minutes

Contains 29 g protein, 30 g carbohydrate, 8 g fat

Season tomato juice with salt and pepper. Spread wheat bread with butter. Top with chicken, catsup and watercress. Accompany all with crispbread.

370 calories

Exotic Breakfast

1 serving

½ cup buttermilk

Liquid non-caloric sweetener

2 kiwis, peeled and diced

2 slices whole-grain rye bread

2 teaspoons whipped butter or margarine

2 plum tomatoes, sliced

Salt and pepper

1 tablespoon chopped chives

15

Grilled Toast

Protein Breakfast

Chicken Sandwich

Holiday Breakfast

Exotic Breakfast

Whole-Grain Bread
with Yogurt

Whole-Grain Bread
with Ham and Cheese

Luxury Breakfast

Orange Cottage Cheese
Breakfast

Preparation: 15 minutes

Contains 12 g protein, 57 g carbohydrate, 10 g fat

Season buttermilk with sweetener. Stir kiwis into milk. Spread bread with butter. Arrange tomato slices on a plate and season with salt and pepper. Sprinkle with chives.

375 calories

Whole-Grain Bread With Ham and Cheese

1 serving

2 slices whole-grain rye bread

2 teaspoons whipped butter or margarine

4 slices (1½ ounces) smoked ham

2 ounces hard cheese, thinly sliced

4 to 6 radishes, thinly sliced

Salt and white pepper

Preparation: 10 minutes

Contains 29 g protein, 42 g carbohydrate, 8 g fat

Spread bread slices with butter. Top one slice with ham and second slice with cheese. Garnish with radishes, seasoned with salt and pepper.

375 calories

Luxury Breakfast

1 serving

½ cup milk

1 tablespoon (packed) brown sugar

1 slice whole-grain wheat bread

1 slice crispbread

2 teaspoons whipped butter or margarine

1 slice (1 ounce) corned beef

Parsley

18

1 hard-cooked egg, sliced

1 teaspoon caviar

Preparation: 10 minutes

Contains 21 g protein, 35 g carbohydrate, 14 g fat

Blend milk with sugar. Spread breads with butter. Top wheat bread with corned beef and garnish with parsley. Place egg slices on crispbread. Spoon caviar in center.

379 calories

Whole-Grain Bread With Yogurt

1 serving

1 cup plain yogurt

1 tablespoon low-calorie marmalade

1 slice whole-grain wheat bread

2 teaspoons whipped butter or margarine

2 ounces (¼ cup) Neuchâtel

2-inch piece of cucumber, sliced

Salt and white pepper

Dill sprigs

1 slice crispbread

Preparation: 15 minutes

Contains 21 g protein, 50 g carbohydrate, 10 g fat

Mix yogurt and marmalade and beat until foamy. Spread wheat bread with butter. Top with cheese and cucumber slices. Sprinkle with salt and pepper. Garnish with dill. Accompany with crispbread.

375 calories

Orange Cottage Cheese Breakfast

1 serving

½ cup skim milk cottage cheese

Liquid non-caloric sweetener

1 orange, peeled, seeded and diced

1 slice whole-grain rye bread

1 slice crispbread

2 teaspoons whipped butter or margarine

1 slice (1 ounce) boiled ham

1 parsley sprig

Preparation: 15 minutes

Contains 27 g protein, 39 g carbohydrate, 7 g fat

Mix cottage cheese with a little water until creamy. Add sweetener to taste. Fold in diced orange. Spread bread slices with butter. Place ham on rye slice and garnish with parsley.

370 calories

Exciting Between-Meal Snacks

These 150-calorie snacks will give you a delicious lift at those times of the day when energy tends to flag. One should be eaten between 10 and 11 in the morning, the other between 4 and 5 in the afternoon. When you divide your daily calorie allotment among five smaller meals a day you are on the best road to reducing.

Roast Beef Crispbread

1 serving

1 slice crispbread

1 slice (1 ounce) roast beef

2 green pepper rings

2 teaspoons cream cheese

Salt and white pepper

Sweet paprika

Preparation: 5 minutes

Contains 12 g protein, 9 g carbohydrate, 8 g fat

Top bread with roast beef. Garnish with pepper rings. Beat cream cheese with a few drops of water until smooth, seasoning with salt, pepper and paprika. Spoon over peppers.

150 calories

German-Style Onion Snack

1 serving

2 ounces Limburger cheese, sliced

¼ cup chopped onion

1 teaspoon herb vinegar

½ teaspoon oil

1 slice crispbread

Preparation: 10 minutes

Contains 19 g protein, 11 g carbohydrate, 29 g fat

Place cheese slices on plate. Top with onion. Sprinkle with vinegar and oil. Serve with crispbread.

160 calories

Viennese Crispbread

1 serving

1 slice crispbread

3 tablespoons cottage cheese

1 small pickle, cut into strips

Salt and white pepper

1 ounce canned Vienna sausage, drained and thinly sliced

Parsley for garnish

Preparation: 5 minutes

Contains 11 g protein, 10 g carbohydrate, 8 g fat

Cover crispbread with cheese. Top with strips of pickle. Sprinkle with salt and pepper. Add sausage slices. Garnish with parsley.

160 calories

Egg Treat

1 serving

½ teaspoon margarine

1 egg

Salt

1 tablespoon chopped chives

5 radishes, sliced

1 slice crispbread

Preparation: 10 minutes

Contains 8 g protein, 10 g carbohydrate, 8 g fat

Melt margarine in small skillet. Add egg and fry until white is firm. Season with salt. Place on plate and sprinkle with chives. Serve with radish slices and crispbread.

160 calories

Cottage Cheese-Tomato Snack

1 serving

1 large plum tomato

3 tablespoons cottage cheese

Salt and sweet paprika

1 small pickle, finely chopped

1 teaspoon chopped chives

2 lettuce leaves

1 slice crispbread

1 teaspoon whipped butter or margarine

Preparation: 15 minutes

Contains 10 g protein, 15 g carbohydrate, 5 g fat

Slice off top of tomato and scoop out seeds and juice. Season cheese with salt and paprika. Stir in pickle. Stuff tomato with cheese mixture and sprinkle with chives. Arrange lettuce leaves on plate and top with tomato. Spread crispbread with butter and serve with tomato.

150 calories

Tartar Crispbread

1 serving

1 slice crispbread

1 teaspoon whipped butter or margarine

2 ounces (¼ cup) very lean ground beef round

Salt and pepper

1 anchovy filet, well drained

1 teaspoon capers

Onion rings

Parsley

Preparation: 5 minutes

21

Contains 16 g protein, 9 g carbohydrate, 4 g fat

Spread crispbread with butter. Place raw beef on top. Sprinkle with salt and pepper. Garnish with anchovy filet, capers, onion rings and parsley.

150 calories

Seasoned Yogurt

1 serving

1 dill pickle, diced

¼ cup chopped onion

1 carrot, coarsely grated

1 cup plain yogurt

1 drop liquid non-caloric sweetener

Salt and pepper

Worcestershire sauce

Parsley

½ slice toast

Preparation: 15 minutes

Contains 11 g protein, 25 g carbohydrate, 1 g fat

Stir pickle, onion and carrot into yogurt. Season with sweetener, salt, pepper and Worcestershire. Place into a bowl and garnish with parsley. Eat with toast.

140 calories

Chicken Nibbles

1 serving

3-inch piece of cucumber, sliced

1 plum tomato, sliced

¼ cup chopped onion

1 tablespoon vinegar

Salt and pepper

Dill sprigs

1 small chicken leg (4 ounces), broiled

½ slice toast

Preparation: 15 minutes

Contains 18 g protein, 12 g carbohydrate, 2 g fat

Combine cucumber, tomato, onion and vinegar. Place on plate. Garnish with dill sprig. Add chicken leg and toast.

150 calories

Garnished Liverwurst Sandwich

1 serving

1 slice toast

1 teaspoon whipped butter or margarine

1 ounce (2 tablespoons) liverwurst

½ teaspoon sharp mustard

¼ cup chopped onion

2 stuffed green olives

Preparation: 10 minutes

Contains 8 g protein, 16 g carbohydrate, 6 g fat

Spread toast with butter. Top with liverwurst. Spread with mustard. Pile on onion. Garnish with olives.

150 calories

Cottage Cheese Piquant

1 serving

¼ cup chopped onion

1 plum tomato, diced

6 tablespoons cottage cheese

Salt and white pepper

Parsley

1 slice crispbread

22

Preparation: 10 minutes

Contains 12 g protein, 14 g carbohydrate, 4 g fat

Combine onion and tomato with cheese. Season with salt and pepper and place on plate. Garnish with parsley. Serve with crispbread.

150 calories

Scrambled Egg

1 serving

1 slice (½ ounce) boiled ham, cut into julienne strips

1 egg

Salt and white pepper

1 tablespoon chopped chives

1 slice crispbread

Preparation: 15 minutes

Contains 11 g protein, 9 g carbohydrate, 8 g fat

Sauté ham in a small skillet until lightly browned. Beat egg with a little water. Season with salt and pepper. Pour egg over ham and stir until moist but firm. Sprinkle with chives. Serve with crispbread.

160 calories

Herbed Cheese Crispbread

1 serving

1 slice crispbread

1 teaspoon whipped butter or margarine

6 tablespoons cottage cheese

Salt and white pepper

1 tablespoon chopped parsley

1 teaspoon chopped chives

3 radishes, cut into julienne strips

1 plum tomato, sliced

Preparation: 10 minutes

Contains 16 g protein, 14 g carbohydrate, 2 g fat

Spread crispbread with butter. Blend cottage cheese with a little water; season with salt and pepper. Stir in parsley and chives. Stir radishes into cheese and place on a plate. (Or spread cheese on crispbread and sprinkle with radishes.) Arrange tomato slices on plate. Sprinkle with salt and pepper and serve with herbed cheese crispbread.

Tip: Try herbed cheese made with a mixture of 1 sprig tarragon, 2 sprigs chervil and 2 tablespoons watercress leaves, all finely chopped. For especially piquant flavor, stir a small plum tomato, seeded and diced, into cheese. Season with salt and pepper.

150 calories

Smoked Salmon Crispbread

1 serving

1 slice crispbread

1 lettuce leaf

1½ ounces smoked salmon

2 teaspoons cream cheese

¼ teaspoon horseradish

1 thin lemon slice

Parsley

Preparation: 5 minutes

Contains 11 g protein, 9 g carbohydrate, 8 g fat

Top crispbread with lettuce, then salmon. Mix cream cheese with a little water and the horseradish. Spoon onto salmon. Add lemon slice and parsley.

150 calories

Blueberry Snack

1 serving

1 cup blueberries, rinsed and well drained

1 cup plain yogurt

23

German-Style Onion Snack

Roast Beef Crispbread

Viennese Crispbread

Egg Treat

Cottage Cheese-Tomato Snack

Tartar Crispbread

Seasoned Yogurt

Garnished Liverwurst
Sandwich

Chicken Nibbles

Cottage Cheese Piquant

Liquid non-caloric sweetener

1 slice crispbread

Preparation: 5 minutes

contains 8 g protein, 29 g carbohydrate, 1 g fat

Mix blueberries with yogurt. Sweeten to taste. Serve with crispbread.

150 calories

Raw Carrot Snack

1 serving

1 cup coarsely grated carrot

1 apple, quartered, cored and grated (do not peel)

1 tablespoon lemon juice

1 drop liquid non-caloric sweetener

2 tablespoons sour cream

1 slice crispbread

Preparation: 15 minutes

Contains 3 g protein, 27 g carbohydrate, 3 g fat

Mix carrot, apple, lemon juice and sweetener. Top with sour cream. Eat with crispbread.

150 calories

Cottage Cheese Cocktail

1 serving

6 tablespoons cottage cheese

1 canned pear half, cut into strips

1 fresh mint leaf

1 slice crispbread

Preparation: 5 minutes

Contains 10 g protein, 20 g carbohydrate, 3 g fat

Place cheese on plate. Top with pear strips. Garnish with mint. Eat with crispbread.

150 calories

Cream Shrimp

1 serving

3½ ounces cooked, shelled and deveined shrimp

1 teaspoon lemon juice

1 tablespoon sour cream

Watercress

1 slice crispbread

Preparation: 5 minutes

Contains 11 g protein, 27 g carbohydrate, 1 g fat

Place shrimp on a plate. Sprinkle with lemon juice. Top with sour cream and garnish with watercress. Serve with crispbread.

140 calories

Spiced Egg

1 serving

1 hard-cooked egg

½ teaspoon each oil and wine vinegar

Salt and white pepper

1 teaspoon sharp mustard

1 slice crispbread

Preparation: 5 minutes

Contains 8 g protein, 9 g carbohydrate, 2 g fat

Shell and halve egg. Remove yolk. Place oil and vinegar in hollows of egg whites. Replace yolks. Season with salt and pepper. Top with mustard. Serve with crispbread.

Tip: The seasoned egg is a bit messy to handle, as the oil and vinegar will run out. It is best to prepare this egg at the table.

160 calories

Fruited Yogurt

1 serving

1 cup strawberries, hulled and halved

1 cup plain yogurt

Liquid non-caloric sweetener

1 slice crispbread

Preparation: 10 minutes

Contains 11 g protein, 27 g carbohydrate, 1 g fat

Mix strawberries with yogurt and sweeten to taste. Serve with crispbread.

150 calories

Melon With Ham

1 serving

1 wedge (6 ounces) honeydew melon, seeded

1 ounce thinly sliced boiled ham

1 slice crispbread

Preparation: 5 minutes

Contains 9 g protein, 20 g carbohydrate, 2 g fat

Place melon wedge on plate. Top with ham. Cover and chill 10 minutes. Serve with crispbread.

150 calories

Raspberry Mix

1 serving

1 cup (5 ounces) raspberries

½ cup milk

1 tablespoon lemon juice

Liquid non caloric sweetener

1 graham cracker

Preparation: 5 minutes

Contains 5 g protein, 24 g carbohydrate, 2 g fat

Puree raspberries in blender with milk and lemon juice. Sweeten to taste. Serve with cracker.

150 calories

Cheese Crispbread

1 serving

1 slice crispbread

1 teaspoon whipped butter or margarine

1 lettuce leaf

2 slices (½ ounce) Edam cheese

1 small plum tomato, sliced

Salt and pepper

Preparation: 5 minutes

Contains 9 g protein, 10 g carbohydrate, 5 g fat

Spread crispbread with butter. Top with lettuce leaf, then cheese slices. Arrange tomato slices on cheese. Season with salt and pepper.

150 calories

Scrambled Egg

Herbed Cheese Crispbread

Blueberry Snack

Smoked Salmon Crispbread

Cottage Cheese Cocktail

Raw Carrot Snack

Cream Shrimp

Spiced Egg

Fruited Yogurt

Melon with Ham

Raspberry Mix

Cheese Crispbread

Take-to-Work Meals

It can be difficult for working people to carry on with a diet. The following recipes will help you to have nourishing and tasty meals on the job—with the right calorie count. All are light and protein-rich, and help to alleviate those midday hunger pangs. Apart from accompaniments, each meal provides 230 to 470 calories. You should, of course, choose your dinner accordingly.

These take-along meals can be prepared the night before and wrapped in foil or plastic wrap. Packing instructions are given so that everything stays fresh: it is important, for example, to pack crispbread separately from other foods, or the bread will soften and taste stale.

Red, White and Green Farmer Cheese

2 servings

8 ounces (1 cup) farmer cheese

2 tablespoons milk

Salt

6 slices whole-grain crispbread

4 teaspoons whipped butter

1/4 cup finely chopped onion

1 plum tomato, sliced

2-inch piece of sliced cucumber

1 dill sprig

1 tablespoon finely chopped chives

1 teaspoon chopped parsley

2 maraschino cherries

1 canned peach half, sliced

1 teaspoon catsup (optional)

Preparation: 20 minutes

Each serving contains 25 g protein, 30 g carbohydrate, 5 g fat

Mix farmer cheese with milk until smooth; add salt to taste. Divide into 3 portions. Butter crispbread. Mix one portion of cheese with onion; spread on 2 crispbreads. Top with tomato and cucumber; garnish with dill. Mix chives and chopped parsley into second portion of cheese; spread on 2 crispbreads. Garnish with cherries. Spread crispbread with remaining cheese; top with peach slices. Add catsup if desired.

To prepare ahead: Pack all ingredients and portions of cheese in separate plastic containers and spread on bread at work.

300 calories per serving

Mexican Salad

2 servings

1 can (4¼ ounces) shrimp, well drained

2 plum tomatoes, peeled and cut into small cubes (½ cup)

¼ cup finely chopped onion

1 cup well drained canned kernel corn (one 8½-ounce can)

1 tablespoon chopped dill

Salt and white pepper

6 ounces (¾ cup) farmer cheese

2 teaspoons oil

1 tablespoon prepared cocktail sauce

Preparation: 15 minutes

Each serving contains 307 calories, 26 g protein, 10 g carbohydrate, 9 g fat

Combine shrimp, tomato, onion, corn and dill. Season with salt and pepper. Mix cheese, oil and cocktail sauce. Season with salt and pepper. Divide shrimp salad between two plates. Serve with cheese mixture.

Accompaniments: Two slices whole-grain rye bread (1½ ounces each), 2 teaspoons butter, 2 slices roast beef (1 ounce each). Each serving contains 173 calories.

To prepare ahead: Place salad and cheese in separate boxes. The bread, spread with butter and topped with roast beef, can be packed in foil.

480 calories per serving

Corned Beef Salad

2 servings

8 ounces corned beef, cut into short strips

4 ounces Edam cheese, cut into short strips

2½ cups chopped celery

2 tablespoons mayonnaise

1 tablespoon catsup

¾ cup plain yogurt

Salt and white pepper (optional)

2 slices crispbread

Preparation: 15 minutes

Each serving contains 44 g protein, 26 g carbohydrate, 20 g fat

Combine corned beef and cheese with celery. Mix mayonnaise, catsup and yogurt until smooth. If necessary, season with salt and pepper. Stir into salad. Accompany with crispbread.

To prepare ahead: Store salad in a tightly closed plastic dish. If you have a refrigerator at work, it will keep best there until ready to eat; otherwise, keep in a cool place. Wrap bread in foil.

470 calories per serving

Thyme Roast Pork

4 servings

1 pound boneless lean pork, in one piece

Salt and white pepper

1 teaspoon dried thyme

2 teaspoons oil

Preparation: 1 hour

31

Red, White and Green Farmer Cheese

Mexican Salad

Corned Beef Salad

Thyme Roast Pork

Stuffed Oranges

**Each serving contains 230 calories,
26 g protein, 0 g carbohydrate, 25 g fat**

Dry pork and rub with salt, pepper and thyme. Heat oil in a skillet and brown pork on all sides for 5 minutes. Add ¼ cup hot water, cover and simmer 45 minutes, adding more water from time to time to prevent drying. Cool pork and cut into four slices. Chill.

To prepare ahead: Wrap 1 slice pork for each serving in foil. Add for each serving 2 medium tomatoes and 1 slice whole-grain wheat bread (1 ounce) spread with 2 teaspoons whipped butter or margarine and wrapped in foil. At work, slice tomatoes and season with onion salt. Next day, take along the remaining 2 slices pork with 1 bunch radishes or 1 medium cucumber per person. Each serving contains 150 calories.

380 calories per serving

Stuffed Oranges

2 servings

1½ cups (8 ounces) strawberries, hulled

2 oranges (6 ounces each)

8 ounces (1 cup) farmer cheese

¼ cup evaporated milk

1 teaspoon cinnamon

1 teaspoon sugar

¼ teaspoon vanilla

Liquid non-caloric sweetener

Preparation: 20 minutes

**Each serving contains 234 calories,
21 g protein, 26 g carbohydrate, 2 g fat**

Cut large berries into quarters; halve small ones. Wash oranges in hot water, dry and cut a slice from top. Scoop out flesh with a sharp knife; reserve shells. Remove membranes from flesh and dice sections. Mix with strawberries. Mix cheese with evaporated milk, cinnamon, sugar and vanilla. Sweeten to taste with liquid sweetener. Mix with fruit and stuff into orange shells. If desired, place lids on top.

Accompaniment: 4 slices rye crispbread. Each serving contains 76 calories.

To prepare ahead: Store the cheese-fruit mixture in a tightly closed plastic box, or stuff oranges in advance and wrap in foil (the cheese will become more aromatic). The stuffed oranges make a good light lunch or between-meal snack.

310 calories per serving

Chinatown Chicken Salad

2 servings

4 dried Chinese mushrooms

2 boneless and skinless chicken breast halves (8 ounces)

4 teaspoons oil

2 tablespoons chicken broth

Salt and white pepper

1 large leek (8 ounces)

2½ cups (5 ounces) bean sprouts

1 can (11 ounces) mandarin oranges, drained (reserve 2 tablespoons juice)

1 tablespoon lemon juice

1 teaspoon ground ginger

2 tablespoons soy sauce

Preparation: 40 minutes

**Each serving contains 332 calories,
33 g protein, 19 g carbohydrate, 11 g fat**

Soak mushrooms in hot water until softened. Cut chicken into strips and sauté in skillet in 2 teaspoons hot oil. Add broth and cook gently 10 minutes. Season with salt and pepper and transfer to bowl to cool. Cut leek into thin strips and clean carefully. Sauté leek with bean sprouts in same skillet. Add to chicken. Discard stems from soaked mushrooms; cut caps into strips. Add to chicken with mandarin oranges. Mix a marinade with remaining 2 teaspoons oil, lemon juice, reserved 2 tablespoons mandarin orange juice, ginger, soy sauce and salt and pepper to taste. Stir into salad and chill.

Accompaniment: 4 slices rye crispbread with 2 teaspoons margarine. Each serving contains 98 calories.

To prepare ahead: Store salad in a plastic box. Wrap crispbread separately in foil; butter at work.

430 calories per serving

Black and White Cheese Strips

2 servings

1 ounce (2 tablespoons) farmer cheese

Salt and white pepper

1 tablespoon chopped parsley

4 slices pumpernickel (1 ounce each)

2 tablespoons whipped margarine

2 slices Edam cheese (1 ounce each)

2 medium tomatoes (8 ounces), sliced

Preparation: 10 minutes

Each serving contains 15 g protein, 34 g carbohydrate, 7 g fat

Mix cheese with salt, pepper and chopped parsley. Spread margarine on one side of pumpernickel slices. Top one slice of pumpernickel with cheese; top with second pumpernickel slice. Press. Spread with cheese mixture. Add another slice of bread buttered side up, a slice of cheese, and remaining slice of bread buttered side down. Press together and cut into four triangles with a sharp knife. Serve with tomato slices.

To prepare ahead: Wrap each triangle in foil and carry tomatoes in plastic bag.

280 calories per serving

Vitamin Sandwich

2 servings

2 tablespoons lemon juice

1 teaspoon oil

Salt and white pepper

2 apples (5 ounces each), cored and sliced

2 cups coarsely grated carrot

3 ounces (6 tablespoons) low fat Cheddar cheese spread

2 slices whole-grain rye bread

2 slices rye toast

Preparation time: 20 minutes

Each serving contains 12 g protein, 57 g carbohydrate, 7 g fat

Mix all but ½ teaspoon lemon juice with oil, salt and pepper. Mix with grated carrots. Toss apple slices with remaining lemon juice. Spread cheese on bread slices and top with apples. Top toast with grated carrots.

To prepare ahead: Pack prepared carrots in foil or in plastic container. Wrap apple slices in foil. Pack cheese and bread separately and prepare at work.

Tip: If you wish, sweeten carrots lightly with liquid non-caloric sweetener.

360 calories per serving

Double Sausage Bread

2 servings

4 slices thin-sliced dark pumpernickel (½ ounce each)

2 teaspoons margarine

2 slices cervelat sausage (½ ounce each)

2 ounces Camembert cheese

1 plum tomato, sliced

2 lettuce leaves

2 apples (5 ounces each)

Preparation: 10 minutes

Each serving contains 10 g protein, 34 g carbohydrate, 14 g fat

Spread bread with margarine. Top 2 slices with cervelat, Camembert and sliced tomatoes. Top each with

35

Black and White Cheese Strips

Chinatown Chicken Salad

Vitamin Sandwich

Double Sausage Bread

Chopped Meat with Eggs

Fruit Kabobs

lettuce leaf and second bread slice. Serve with apples.

To prepare ahead: Pack sandwich and apple separately in plastic wrap or boxes.

330 calories per serving

Fruit Kabobs

2 servings

2 apples (5 ounces each), cored and thinly sliced

1 tablespoon lemon juice

2 oranges (6 ounces each), peeled and sliced

¾ cup (4 ounces) green grapes

4 slices whole-grain wheat bread (1 ounce each)

4 teaspoons whipped margarine

4 slices Edam cheese (½ ounce each)

2 cups tomato juice

Preparation: 15 minutes

Each serving contains 15 g protein, 69 g carbohydrate, 10 g fat

Sprinkle apple slices with lemon juice. Spear apples, orange slices and grapes on skewers. Spread bread with margarine and top with cheese. Serve both with tomato juice.

To prepare ahead: Wrap kabobs in foil. Spread bread with margarine, top with cheese and take along in plastic bags.

440 calories per serving

Chopped Meat With Eggs

4 servings

8 ounces ground beef round

8 ounces ground veal

½ cup finely chopped onion

6 tablespoons dry breadcrumbs

2 tablespoons cold water

2 eggs

Salt and pepper

1 teaspoon dried thyme

1 teaspoon paprika

2 tablespoons chopped parsley

2 hard-cooked eggs

2 tablespoons oil

1 cup chicken broth

Preparation: 1¼ hours

Each serving contains 388 calories, 28 g protein, 7 g carbohydrate, 26 g fat

Preheat oven to 350°F. Mix meats with onion, crumbs, water, eggs, salt, pepper, thyme, paprika and parsley. Knead until well blended and press into an oblong. Place eggs in the middle. Wrap meat around eggs and shape into a loaf. Heat 1 tablespoon oil in a shallow baking pan on top of stove. Brown meat on all sides. Brush with remaining oil and bake for 50 minutes, spooning broth over loaf several times during baking. Cool and cut loaf into 8 slices.

Accompaniment (2 servings): Salad made with 1 small head Boston lettuce, 1 medium tomato and 1 small cucumber, tossed with a vinaigrette using 2 teaspoons oil. Each serving contains 82 calories.

To prepare ahead: Wrap meat slices in foil. Pack salad separately, adding dressing at work.

470 calories per serving

Indian Chicken

2 servings

2 chicken legs (12 ounces)

4 teaspoons oil

¼ cup chopped onion

¼ cup dry white wine

1 tablespoon curry powder

Pepper

1 tablespoon mango chutney

1 tablespoon chopped parsley

¼ cup sour cream

Preparation: 30 minutes, without marinating time

Each serving contains 342 calories, 28 g protein, 13 g carbohydrate, 17 g fat

Pat chicken dry. Heat oil in a skillet and sauté onion until golden brown. Add wine, cover and simmer 3 minutes. Remove from heat. Stir in curry powder, pepper, chutney and parsley. Add chicken and turn to coat. Cover and refrigerate overnight. The next day, remove chicken, reserving marinade. Cook chicken legs in a skillet or under a moderate broiler for 40 to 45 minutes. Bring marinade to boil; cool. Stir into sour cream. Season to taste and serve with chicken. Eat hot or cold.

Accompaniment: 2 slices rye crispbread. Each serving contains 38 calories.

To prepare ahead: Wrap chicken in foil; pack sour cream mixture separately.

380 calories per serving

Mushroom Pockets Jana

4 servings (makes 12 pockets)

Half of one 17¼-ounce package frozen puff pastry sheets

1 strip lean bacon, finely chopped

½ cup finely chopped onion

1 can (4 ounces) sliced mushrooms, drained

1 tablespoon tomato paste

Seasoned salt and white pepper

2 teaspoons butter

1 tablespoon flour

1 egg yolk

¼ cup evaporated milk

Preparation: 1 hour

Each serving contains 412 calories, 7 g protein, 29 g carbohydrate, 11 g fat

Thaw 1 sheet of puff pastry for 20 minutes. Sauté bacon and onion until golden brown. Add mushrooms. Stir in tomato paste, salt, pepper and butter and cook until all liquid has evaporated. Cool. Unfold pastry and cut into 12 two-inch rounds. Divide filling among rounds. Brush edges of dough with water, fold over and press edges together. Place on ungreased cookie sheets. Beat egg yolk with evaporated milk and brush onto turnovers. Prick tops with a fork. Let turnovers rest 15 minutes. Preheat oven to 400°F. Bake turnovers until golden brown, about 20 minutes.

Accompaniment: 3 medium or 6 plum tomatoes. Each serving contains 38 calories.

To prepare ahead: Wrap 3 turnovers in foil and take along 3 plum tomatoes for each serving.

450 calories per serving

Pizza Burgers

2 servings

3 tablespoons dry breadcrumbs

8 ounces ground beef round

¼ cup finely chopped onion

1 egg

Salt

1 tablespoon sweet paprika

Pinch of cayenne pepper

1 tablespoon chili sauce

2 teaspoons oil

1 hard-cooked egg, sliced

1 small tomato, sliced

5 stuffed green olives, sliced

4 anchovy filets, drained

2 slices Edam cheese (½ ounce each), cut into strips

39

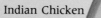

Indian Chicken

Mushroom Pockets Jana

Pizza Burgers

Farm Chicken Salad

Gourmet Cabbage Rolls

Catalonian Rice Salad

Preparation: 25 minutes

**Each serving contains 430 calories,
41 g protein, 15 g carbohydrate, 19 g fat**

Preheat oven to 425°F. Soak crumbs in a little water. Mix with ground meat, onion, raw egg, salt, paprika, cayenne and chili sauce. Shape into 2 flat hamburgers. Heat oil in a skillet and fry burgers on both sides for 5 minutes. Transfer to cookie sheet. Place hard-cooked egg, tomato and olives on hamburgers. Top with anchovies and cheese and bake for 10 minutes.

Accompaniments: Salad of 1 medium cucumber, sliced and tossed with vinegar dressing; 2 slices rye crispbread. Each serving contains 50 calories.

Prepare ahead: Wrap cold pizza burgers in foil; carry salad in a plastic box.

480 calories per serving

Farm Chicken Salad

2 servings

6 ounces frozen peas (⅔ of one 10-ounce package)

Salt

6 ounces celery root

1 teaspoon lemon juice

1 celery heart (6 ounces)

1 dill pickle, cut into strips

*8 ounces cooked skinned and boned chicken,
cut into chunks*

2 ounces (¼ cup) farmer cheese

2 tablespoons herb vinegar

White pepper

2 teaspoons oil

Preparation: 40 minutes

**Each serving contains 340 calories,
38 g protein, 19 g carbohydrate, 10 g fat**

Cook peas according to package directions. Drain and cool. Peel celery root. Cut into thin slices, then

cut slices into thin strips. Place in a bowl and sprinkle with lemon juice. Cut celery heart into pieces. Add to celery root with pickle and chicken. Mix cheese until smooth. Stir into salad. Let marinate 10 minutes, then adjust seasoning.

Accompaniment: 2 slices whole-grain wheat bread (1 ounce each), 2 teaspoons whipped butter. Each serving contains 110 calories.

To prepare ahead: Cover salad and refrigerate overnight. If possible, store in refrigerator at work.

450 calories

Catalonian Rice Salad

2 servings

5 tablespoons long-grain rice

Salt

½ cup (4 ounces) canned carrots, drained

1 medium-size red pepper, cut into strips

3 plum tomatoes, peeled and diced

3 drops Tabasco

1 hard-cooked egg

1 garlic clove, finely chopped

1 egg

1 teaspoon mustard

1 teaspoon herb vinegar

Liquid non-caloric sweetener

4 ounces (½ cup) farmer cheese

2 teaspoons oil

White pepper

Preparation: 30 minutes

**Each serving contains 23 g protein,
36 g carbohydrate, 12 g fat**

Cook rice in salted water 15 minutes; drain. Cook peas in boiling salted water 6 to 8 minutes; drain. Combine rice, peas, carrots, red pepper and tomato with Tabasco and let marinate. Transfer to serving bowl and garnish with egg slices. Combine garlic, raw egg, mustard, herb vinegar, liquid sweetener and cheese. Stir in oil and season with salt and pepper. Serve cheese mixture with salad.

To prepare ahead: Salad and cheese mixture should be packed separately in tight containers. Accompany with a small broiled chicken leg if you wish; 4 ounces cooked chicken contains 144 calories.

362 calories per serving

Gourmet Cabbage Rolls

2 servings

8 large cabbage leaves

Salt

1 can (6½ ounces) tuna packed in oil, drained

½ cup chopped onion

2 teaspoons oil

6 tablespoons dry breadcrumbs

White pepper

1 egg

1 cup plain yogurt

1 tablespoon sweet paprika

1 teaspoon sharp mustard

Preparation: 30 minutes

**Each serving contains 375 calories,
25 g protein, 26 g carbohydrate, 19 g fat**

Cook the cabbage leaves in boiling salted water for 5 minutes. Remove leaves, reserving liquid. Cut away thick ribs and cut leaves in half. Puree drained tuna in a blender or food processor. Sauté onion in oil for 2 to 3 minutes. Add crumbs and pepper and remove from heat. Stir in tuna puree and egg. Shape into 16 small balls and wrap each ball in a half cabbage leaf. Arrange in large saucepan and just cover with some of the reserved cabbage cooking water. Simmer over low heat 20 minutes. Mix a sauce of yogurt, paprika, mustard and salt and pepper to taste. Remove cabbage rolls from pot with a slotted spoon, place into a bowl and top with yogurt sauce.

Accompaniment: 2 slices toast. Each serving contains 65 calories.

To prepare ahead: Place cabbage rolls and sauce in plastic box and seal well. Take along 1 slice rye crispbread; it contains 27 fewer calories than 1 slice toast.

440 calories per serving

43

For Soup Lovers

A group of nutrition researchers conducted an experiment with happy results for all soup lovers: Soup as a first course acts as an appetite suppressant, since it provides strong feelings of satisfaction. Naturally, you will not automatically become thin by eating soup. But it helps to overcome hunger pangs so that you do not eat the rest of the meal in uncontrollable amounts.

Here you will find five really delicious soups that contain between 160 and 180 calories. If you do not want to go above your daily allowance, choose one of the lower-calorie entrees, omit the accompaniments or skip a snack. Most commercially prepared soups contain between 45 and 85 calories, so you can eat a portion between meals on a reducing diet.

Chinese-Style Vegetable Bouillon

2 servings

3½ ounces lean boneless beef

2 tablespoons soy sauce

1 teaspoon flour

Salt and pepper

1 teaspoon oil

2 cups hot clear beef broth (made from bouillon cubes)

1 small carrot, cut into thin strips

2 cups (3½ ounces) bean sprouts

6 medium mushrooms, sliced

½ ounce transparent noodles, cut into short lengths

3½ ounces spinach leaves

1 tablespoon dry sherry

Preparation: 40 minutes

Each serving contains 16 g protein, 10 g carbohydrate, 6 g fat

Cut beef into paper-thin strips. Mix 1 tablespoon soy sauce with flour, salt and pepper. Mix with beef and let stand 10 minutes. Heat oil in a saucepan. Fry beef with marinade on all sides. Add the heated beef broth. Add carrot strips and simmer 5 minutes. Add the sprouts, sliced mushrooms and noodles to the soup. Stir and cook another 5 minutes. Add spinach and heat briefly. Season with remaining soy sauce, sherry, salt and pepper.

180 calories per serving

Gazpacho Andaluse

2 servings

1 red and 1 small green pepper

¼ cup coarsely chopped onion

1 garlic clove

1 tablespoon oil

1 teaspoon dry breadcrumbs

Salt

2 small tomatoes, peeled and chopped

¾ cup coarsely diced cucumber

1 tablespoon lemon juice

5 tablespoons cold water

White pepper

Pinch of cayenne pepper

1 slice toast or zwieback

2 teaspoons margarine

Preparation: 25 minutes, without chilling time

Each serving contains 4 g protein, 21 g carbohydrate, 9 g fat

Quarter peppers; remove seeds. Cut into large squares. Finely chop some of each pepper and onion until you have 1 tablespoon each. Set aside. Puree remaining onion, pepper, garlic, oil, breadcrumbs and salt in a blender. Finely chop 1 tablespoon of tomato and cucumber each and set aside. Add remainder to blender and puree. Stir in lemon juice and water.

Season with salt, pepper and cayenne. Chill for 30 minutes. Dice toast. Sauté in hot margarine until crisp. Divide soup between two plates. Garnish with reserved finely chopped vegetables and bread cubes.

180 calories per serving

Paprika Goulash Soup

2 servings

1 teaspoon oil

3½ ounces boneless beef, cut into small cubes

2 tablespoons chopped onion

Salt and pepper

1½ cups hot clear beef broth (made from bouillon cubes)

1 small to medium-size green pepper, seeded and cut into strips

1 tablespoon sweet paprika

1 medium tomato, peeled, seeded and diced

1 tablespoon finely chopped parsley

Preparation: 45 minutes

Each serving contains 12 g protein, 6 g carbohydrate, 9 g fat

Heat oil in a pot. Brown beef and onion. Season lightly with salt and pepper. Add beef broth and simmer, covered, for 20 minutes. Add pepper strips and paprika and cook 10 minutes. Add tomato and cook 5 more minutes. Adjust seasoning and sprinkle with parsley.

Tip: If you enjoy garlic, chop ½ garlic clove and sauté with onion.

178 calories per serving

Pea Soup With Shrimp

2 servings

1 teaspoon margarine

2 tablespoons finely chopped onion

1 carrot, finely chopped

45

1½ cups hot clear beef broth (made from bouillon cubes)

3½ ounces frozen baby peas (⅓ of one 10-ounce package)

3½ ounces cooked, shelled and deveined shrimp

½ cup plus 2 tablespoons dry white wine

1 tablespoon sour cream

Salt and pepper

1 tablespoon chopped parsley

Preparation: 35 minutes

Each serving contains 14 g protein, 10 g carbohydrate, 4 g fat

Melt margarine in a saucepan. Sauté onion and carrot for 5 minutes. Add beef broth and cook 10 minutes. Add frozen peas and cook 8 minutes. Add shrimp and white wine and bring to boil. Stir in sour cream. Season with salt and pepper. Serve soup sprinkled with parsley.

Tip: This soup has a delicious, unusual flavor when seasoned with curry powder.

180 calories per serving

Italian Tomato Soup

2 servings

½ garlic clove, chopped

1½ pounds tomatoes

1 tablespoon oil

¼ cup chopped onion

Salt and white pepper

Pinch each of rosemary and thyme

2 cups hot clear beef broth (made from bouillon cubes)

1 ounce Parmesan cheese, grated (¼ cup)

Preparation: 50 minutes

Each serving contains 7 g protein, 14 g carbohydrate, 6 g fat

Coarsely chop all but one of the tomatoes. Heat oil in a large saucepan and sauté onion and garlic until golden brown. Add chopped tomatoes and sauté 5 minutes. Season with salt, pepper, rosemary and thyme. Add hot beef broth and cook uncovered for 20 minutes. In the meantime, dip reserved tomato into boiling water for a few seconds, then into cold water. Peel, core and dice. Put soup through a sieve or food mill, or puree in food processor. Return to saucepan and add tomato cubes. Reheat soup and serve. Sprinkle with cheese.

160 calories per serving

Gourmet Lunches and Dinners

Each of these meals contains, apart from accompaniments, 140 to 160 calories. The range is deliberately broad to accommodate individual tastes—whether you prefer your main meal in the evening or at midday, whether you'd like to add soup or dessert, and so on.

Keep in mind that breakfast and two snacks provide about 675 calories per day. Therefore, if you are sticking to 1500 calories, lunch and dinner combined should total about 825. Choose your recipes accordingly: if you select two of the lower-calorie meals in one day you may have room for extras, perhaps one of the 100-calorie snacks (see pages 93 to 96). You can also set a more ambitious goal—say, 1200 calories—and again select recipes to suit.

All of these recipes make two servings, and most include suggestions for accompaniments. You can adjust the accompaniment as necessary to limit your day's calorie quota, or for fastest results you can omit it altogether.

Cheese-Stuffed Pepper Rings

2 servings

2 large red or green peppers

8 ounces (1 cup) farmer cheese

1 tablespoon grated Parmesan cheese

1 tablespoon wheat germ

Salt and pepper

1 tablespoon chopped parsley

1 tablespoon chives

Preparation: 15 minutes, without chilling

Each serving contains 174 calories, 22 g protein, 12 g carbohydrate, 6 g fat

Cut tops from peppers. Remove seeds, wash and pat dry inside and out. Mix farmer cheese with Parmesan and wheat germ. Season to taste with salt and pepper. Stir in chopped herbs. Pack tightly into peppers. Wrap in foil and chill 2 hours. At serving time, cut peppers crosswise into thick slices.
Accompaniment: 2 slices pumpernickel (1 ounce each) spread with 2 teaspoons butter, ¾ cup (4 ounces) grapes, 10 stuffed green olives. Each serving contains 176 calories.

350 calories per serving

Chinese-Style Vegetable Bouillon

Gazpacho Andaluse

Paprika Goulash Soup

Pea Soup with Shrimp

Italian Tomato Soup

Sicilian Tomatoes

2 servings

2 small tomatoes

4 anchovy filets, drained and chopped

2 dill gherkins, finely chopped

1 hard-cooked egg

Salt and white pepper

1 teaspoon wine vinegar

2 teaspoons oil

1 tablespoon chopped chives

2 stuffed green olives

4 Boston lettuce leaves

Preparation: 20 minutes

**Each serving contains 140 calories,
7 g protein, 4 g carbohydrate, 10 g fat**

Wash and dry tomatoes. Cut a slice off top of each and hollow out tomatoes. Chop the "lid" and remove pulp and transfer to bowl. Add the chopped anchovies and pickles. Cut 2 wedges from egg. Chop remaining egg and add to bowl. Season mixture with salt and pepper. Mix vinegar, oil and chives; season to taste with salt and pepper. Stir into bowl. Use mixture to stuff tomatoes. Place lettuce leaves on two plates. Top with tomatoes. Garnish with egg wedges and sliced olives.

Accompaniments: 2 slices toast spread with 2 teaspoons butter, 2 slices cooked ham (2 ounces each). Each serving contains 290 calories.

430 calories per serving

Soy Leeks and Mushrooms

2 servings

2 large leeks (1 pound)

1½ cups beef broth (made from bouillon cubes)

Salt and white pepper

1 tablespoon lemon juice

Half of one 4-ounce can mushrooms, chopped

2 ounces Cheddar cheese, cut into thin strips

1 tablespoon soy sauce

3 tablespoons cream

Nutmeg

Preparation: 30 minutes

**Each serving contains 235 calories,
11 g protein, 18 g carbohydrate, 11 g fat**

Cut upper green leaves from leeks, leaving only the pale green portion. Halve leeks lengthwise; if very long, cut in half crosswise. Wash leeks carefully to remove sand from between layers. Place broth in saucepan. Add leeks and salt lightly. Season with pepper and lemon juice. Cover and simmer 20 minutes, adding mushrooms just before end of cooking time. Add cheese to hot pan juices and stir until melted. Stir in soy sauce and cream. Season with nutmeg, salt and pepper and serve.

Accompaniments: 4 lean grilled slices pork loin (2 ounces each) with 2 small boiled potatoes (8 ounces). Each serving contains 305 calories.

540 calories per serving

Greek Carrot Plaki

2 servings

1 pound carrots, cut into julienne

Salt and sweet paprika

White pepper

4 teaspoons oil

½ cup chopped onion

3 tablespoons finely chopped parsley

Preparation: 40 minutes

**Each serving contains 202 calories,
3 g protein, 21 g carbohydrate, 10 g fat**

Season carrot julienne with salt, paprika and pepper. Heat oil in skillet and sauté onion. Add carrot strips and 2 tablespoons of the chopped parsley. Pour in 1 cup hot water, cover and simmer 40 minutes. Serve sprinkled with remaining parsley.

50

Accompaniment: 2 broiled lean beef filet mignons (4 ounces each). Each serving contains 158 calories.

360 calories per serving

Boiled Potatoes With Herbed Cheese

2 servings

1 pound new potatoes

Salt

8 ounces (1 cup) farmer cheese

5 tablespoons sour cream

½ cup chopped onion

Sweet paprika

Pepper

1 bunch chives

½ bunch parsley

1 hard-cooked egg, chopped

Preparation: 40 minutes

Each serving contains 365 calories, 26 g protein, 45 g carbohydrate, 7 g fat

Boil potatoes in salted water to cover for 30 minutes. Mix cheese with sour cream in a bowl. Stir in onion. Season to taste with salt, paprika and pepper. Chop chives and parsley. Stir herbs into cheese, reserving 1 teaspoon chives. Stir in egg. Serve cheese with potatoes. Garnish with reserved chives.

Accompaniments: Salad of 3 medium tomatoes in a vinegar dressing made with desired herbs, ¼ cup chopped onion and 1 tablespoon chopped chives. Each serving contains 35 calories.

400 calories per serving

Stuffed Pepper Apple

2 servings

2 apples (6 ounces each)

1 tablespoon lemon juice

2 plum tomatoes, diced

2 mustard pickles (4 ounces), diced

¼ cup finely chopped onion

1 tablespoon green peppercorns

Salt and lemon pepper

1 tablespoon cider vinegar

4 teaspoons soy oil

Preparation: 30 minutes

Each serving contains 215 calories, 2 g protein, 27 g carbohydrate, 10 g fat

Cut a slice from top of each apple. Scoop out apple with a knife until only a thin shell remains. Sprinkle shell with some of the lemon juice. Dice apple removed, discarding core. Mix with remaining lemon juice, tomatoes, pickles, onion and green peppercorns. Season with salt and lemon pepper. Let stand 10 minutes. Taste and adjust seasoning. Fill apple shells; serve extra salad on plate.

Accompaniment: 7 ounces low-fat cheese, 2 slices whole-grain crispbread. Each serving contains 185 calories.

400 calories per serving

Gourmet Stuffed Celery Root

2 servings

6 small celery roots (1 pound)

2 plum tomatoes, peeled and diced

2 ounces cooked tongue, chopped (⅓ cup)

1 slice canned pineapple, chopped

1 tablespoon sliced almonds

1 tablespoon catsup

Salt and white pepper

4 teaspoons oil

1 cup hot chicken broth (made from bouillon cubes)

51

Sicilian Tomatoes

Garlic Veal Steak

Herbed Cheese Cake

Mushroom Mustard Cutlet

Smoked Salmon Salad

Egg in Casserole

1 tablespoon chopped parsley

¼ cup cream

1 tablespoon soy flour

Preparation: 1 hour

**Each serving contains 423 calories,
15 g protein, 30 g carbohydrate, 25 g fat**

Peel celery roots and scoop out the center of each. Finely dice the part removed and mix with tomatoes, tongue, pineapple, almonds and catsup. Season with salt and pepper. Stuff mixture into celery roots. Heat oil in Dutch oven and sauté celery roots for 10 minutes. Add hot broth, cover and simmer 20 minutes. Transfer celery roots to bowl and sprinkle with parsley. Mix cream with soy flour, stir into pan juices and stir constantly until thickened. Season to taste. Serve sauce with celery roots.

Accompaniment: 2 small boiled potatoes (8 ounces). Each serving contains 87 calories.

510 calories per serving

Delicate Asparagus Omelet With Shrimp

2 servings

12 ounces asparagus (canned white or frozen and thawed green, drained)

4 teaspoons butter

4 ounces frozen shelled and deveined shrimp, thawed

Salt and white pepper

2 tablespoons flour

2 tablespoons milk

2 eggs

Parsley for garnish

Preparation: 20 minutes

**Each serving contains 286 calories,
21 g protein, 11 g carbohydrate, 75 g fat**

Cut asparagus into 1-inch lengths. Melt 1 tablespoon of the butter in saucepan. Add asparagus and heat 5 minutes. Add shrimp and heat another 5 minutes; keep warm. Season to taste with salt and pepper. Mix flour and milk. Add eggs and whisk thoroughly. Add 1 tablespoon cold water and beat again. Season with salt and pepper. In nonstick pan, prepare two omelets using remaining 1 teaspoon butter. Place on warmed plates. Top with hot asparagus mixture and fold omelets over filling. Garnish with parsley sprigs.

Accompaniments: Salad of 2 small heads Boston lettuce in a dressing made with vinegar, desired herbs, 1 tablespoon chopped chives and 2 teaspoons oil. Each serving contains 64 calories.

350 calories per serving

Farmer's Omelet

2 servings

1 strip lean bacon, finely chopped

1 pound potatoes, cooked, peeled and sliced

Salt

2 eggs

2 tablespoons skim milk

2 medium tomatoes, peeled and diced

1 tablespoon chopped chives

Preparation: 25 minutes

**Each serving contains 14 g protein,
42 g carbohydrate, 16 g fat**

Cook bacon in a skillet. Add potato slices and salt and cook until golden brown. Beat eggs with skim milk; salt lightly. Stir tomatoes and chives into eggs. Pour mixture over potatoes and cook 10 minutes without stirring. Cut omelet in half and serve on two warmed plates.

Tip: This farmer's omelet takes on a Hungarian flavor when 2 medium-size green or red peppers, cut into strips (parboiled for 2 minutes, then drained) are substituted for the tomatoes.

375 calories per serving

54

Colorful Omelet

2 servings

2 teaspoons butter or margarine

1 garlic clove, chopped

¼ cup chopped onion

1 green pepper, seeded and cut into strips

3 plum tomatoes, peeled and diced

Salt and pepper

2 tablespoons sour cream

2 eggs

Preparation: 30 minutes

**Each serving contains 186 calories,
9 g protein, 8 g carbohydrate, 12 g fat**

Melt butter in nonstick skillet and sauté garlic and onion until golden brown. Add pepper strips and sauté 5 minutes. Stir in tomatoes. Season with salt and pepper, cover and cook 10 minutes. Stir in sour cream. Beat eggs and pour over vegetables. Sprinkle with a little salt. Cook omelet 5 minutes without stirring. Serve in pan, allowing half of omelet per serving.

Accompaniments: 4 slices rye crispbread, 4 slices cooked ham (4 ounces). Each serving contains 174 calories.

360 calories per serving

Stuffed Herb Omelet

2 servings

8 ounces fresh mushrooms, sliced

Salt

8 ounces frozen peas

White pepper

Onion powder

4 teaspoons margarine

2 tablespoons chopped parsley

4 eggs

Preparation: 30 minutes

**Each serving contains 24 g protein,
16 g carbohydrate, 20 g fat**

Cook mushrooms in a little salted water for 10 minutes. Cook peas in boiling salted water for 8 minutes. Drain vegetables, mix and season with white pepper and onion powder. Stir in 1 teaspoon margarine and 1 tablespoon chopped parsley. Melt remaining 1 tablespoon margarine in a skillet. Pour in half of the egg mixture, tilting skillet so egg covers pan evenly. Cook without stirring for 3 minutes; top should still be creamy. Slide omelet out of pan onto warmed plate. Spoon half of filling onto omelet and fold over. Prepare second omelet in the same way.

370 calories per serving

Egg in Casserole

2 servings

2 eggs

2 teaspoons margarine

¼ cup sliced onion

1 green pepper, seeded and cut into strips

2 plum tomatoes, sliced

2 ounces sliced ham, cut into strips

Salt and white pepper

½ cup milk

1 tablespoon flour

2 ounces (¼ cup) Cheddar cheese spread

1 tablespoon chopped chives

Preparation: 35 minutes

**Each serving contains 321 calories,
20 g protein, 16 g carbohydrate, 18 g fat**

Cook eggs for 6 minutes; shell. Grease 2 individual casseroles with some of the margarine. Melt remaining margarine in skillet and fry onion slices until golden brown. Add pepper and tomatoes and cook 5 minutes. Toss in ham. Season to taste with salt and pepper. Spoon into casseroles. Add one egg to each casserole. Preheat oven to 400°F. Beat milk

55

Baked Veal Cutlet

Stuffed Artichoke Bottoms

Delicate Leek Toast

Farmer's Omelet

Boiled Potatoes with Herbed Cheese

with flour. Heat, stirring, until thickened. Stir in cheese until melted. Stir in chives. Pour sauce over eggs. Bake until golden, about 10 to 15 minutes.

Accompaniments: Salad of 2 medium-size sliced tomatoes in a vinegar dressing with desired herbs, ¼ cup chopped onion and 1 tablespoon chopped chives; 2 slices whole-grain crispbread. Each serving contains 69 calories.

390 calories per serving

Herbed Cheese Cakes

2 servings

12 ounces boiling potatoes (3 small), boiled and cooled

6 ounces (¾ cup) farmer cheese

1 egg

1 tablespoon flour

Salt and white pepper

1 tablespoon tomato paste

1 tablespoon each chopped parsley, chives and chervil

1 teaspoon chopped tarragon

3½ ounces lean corned beef, finely chopped

2 teaspoons oil

Preparation: 40 minutes

Each serving contains 367 calories, 31 g protein, 29 g carbohydrate, 12 g fat

Peel potatoes and shred. Stir cheese in a bowl until smooth. Stir in potatoes, then egg and flour. Season with salt and pepper and tomato paste. Stir in herbs and corned beef. Heat oil in a skillet. Shape potato mixture into cakes. Fry until crisp, about 6 minutes per side.

Accompaniments: Salad of 1 medium cucumber (8 ounces) in a vinegar dressing with ¼ cup chopped onion, 1 tablespoon chopped parsley and a drop or two of liquid non-caloric sweetener; two 8-ounce glasses tomato juice. Each serving contains 63 calories.

430 calories per serving

Amsterdam Corned Beef Salad

2 servings

8 ounces green beans, broken into pieces

Salt and pepper

1 medium-large tomato, skinned and coarsely diced

2 ounces Edam cheese, cut into short strips

6 ounces lean corned beef, diced

1 to 2 tablespoons red wine vinegar

4 teaspoons oil

1 tablespoon chopped chives

1 tablespoon chopped parsley

Pinch of dried marjoram

Watercress for garnish

Preparation: 50 minutes, without marinating time

Each serving contains 336 calories, 26 g protein, 10 g carbohydrate, 19 g fat

Cook beans in small amount of water in saucepan until crisp-tender. Season with salt and pepper. Drain and chill. Combine beans with tomato, cheese and corned beef. Mix vinegar with salt and pepper to taste in small bowl. Stir in 1 tablespoon water. Beat in oil. Add to salad ingredients with chives, parsley and marjoram and toss well. Let marinate 10 minutes. Adjust seasoning and serve garnished with watercress.

Accompaniment: 2 slices whole-grain wheat bread (1 ounce each). Each serving contains 74 calories.

410 calories per serving

Stuffed Artichoke Bottoms

2 servings

6 ounces lean ground beef round

½ cup finely chopped onion

1 egg

Salt and pepper

1 tablespoon chopped parsley

4 canned artichoke bottoms, drained

1 tablespoon grated Parmesan cheese

1 teaspoon oil

Preparation: 20 minutes

**Each serving contains 210 calories,
19 g protein, 9 g carbohydrate, 7 g fat**

Position rack to center of oven and preheat to 425°F. Grease baking sheet. Combine ground meat, onion and egg. Season with salt, pepper and parsley. Fill drained artichoke bottoms with meat mixture. Sprinkle with cheese. Place on prepared baking sheet and bake until meat is cooked, about 10 minutes.

Accompaniment: 2 slices whole-grain wheat bread (1 ounce each), 2 teaspoons butter. Each serving contains 110 calories.

Tip: If you are fond of Beef Tartare, try these stuffed artichoke bottoms raw.

320 calories per serving

California Steak

2 servings

4 teaspoons oil

2 beef filet steaks (4 ounces each)

Salt and white pepper

2 canned pear halves, drained

Sweet paprika

1 tablespoon coarsely chopped walnuts

Watercress to garnish

Preparation: 15 minutes

**Each serving contains 326 calories,
25 g protein, 10 g carbohydrate, 18 g fat**

Heat oil in skillet over high heat. Pat steaks dry with paper towels. Brown steaks 30 seconds on each side in hot oil, then sauté 2 to 3 more minutes on each side. Season with salt and pepper and transfer to heated platter; keep warm. Place pears in skillet and heat through. Place on steaks. Dust lightly with paprika and sprinkle with walnuts. Serve steaks garnished with watercress.

Accompaniment: 5 tablespoons raw long-grain rice, cooked and seasoned with salt and paprika. Each serving contains 114 calories.

440 calories per serving

Flamed Pepper Steak

2 servings

2 filet mignons (4 ounces each)

Salt

1 heaping tablespoon green peppercorns

4 teaspoons butter

2 teaspoons oil

2 tablespoons Cognac

2 tablespoons water

1 tablespoon tomato paste

Preparation: 20 minutes

**Each serving contains 327 calories,
26 g protein, 5 g carbohydrate, 18 g fat**

Sprinkle steaks with salt on both sides. Mix peppercorns with butter, mashing peppercorns. Spread mixture on both sides of steaks. Heat oil in a skillet over high heat. Brown steaks 30 seconds on each side, then cook 3 minutes on each side to finish. Place Cognac in a ladle and warm. Set steaks on heated plates. Flame Cognac and pour, still flaming, over steaks. Mix water with tomato paste. Add to pan in which steaks were cooked and bring to a boil, scraping up browned bits. Season sauce and pour over steaks.

Accompaniments: 1 large tomato, halved, topped with 1 tablespoon grated Parmesan cheese and broiled; 2 slices rye crispbread. Each serving contains 83 calories.

410 calories per serving

59

Ham with Melon, Roman Style

Garden Turkey Salad

Colorful Omelet

Stuffed Herb Omelet

Stuffed Pepper Apple

Amsterdam Corned Beef Salad

Paprika Steak

2 servings

2 teaspoons oil

2 filet mignons (4 ounces each), pounded to flatten

1 small onion, sliced

Salt

2 teaspoons green peppercorns

1 green pepper, cut into rings

4 ounces canned or thawed frozen artichoke hearts, drained

Sweet paprika

Preparation: 20 minutes

Each serving contains 260 calories, 26 g protein, 10 g carbohydrate, 10 g fat

Heat oil in skillet over high heat and fry steaks 30 seconds on each side. Add onion and cook steaks 2 to 3 minutes more on each side, allowing onions to become golden brown. Season steaks with salt, transfer to platter and keep warm. Add green peppercorns, pepper rings and artichoke hearts to pan juices and sauté 10 minutes. Season with salt and paprika. Spoon mixture in skillet over steaks.

Accompaniments: Salad made from 1 small head Boston lettuce, 1 bunch radishes and ¼ cup sliced onion marinated in ¼ cup white wine vinegar (no oil). Also, 1 cup cooked peas with 2 teaspoons butter, and 2 small boiled potatoes (eight ounces). Each serving contains 270 calories.

530 calories per serving

Tournedos With Tomatoes

2 servings

2 teaspoons butter

2 plum tomatoes, peeled, seeded and diced

Salt and pepper

Sweet paprika

1 tablespoon chopped parsley

2 teaspoons oil

4 slices filet mignon (tournedos), 2 ounces each

Garlic salt

Preparation: 20 minutes

Each serving contains 246 calories, 23 g protein, 2 g carbohydrate, 14 g fat

Melt 1 teaspoon of the butter in a skillet and sauté tomatoes 5 minutes. Season with salt, pepper and paprika. Stir in chopped parsley. Heat oil in another skillet. Pound filet slices to ¼-inch thickness. Season with pepper and garlic salt. Sauté for 2 minutes on each side. Add remaining 1 teaspoon butter to skillet and cook for 1 minute. Place meat on warmed plates. Spoon sautéed tomatoes on top.

Accompaniments: Salad made of 1 pound cooked, cooled asparagus dressed with ½ cup sour cream, salt and curry powder; also, 8 ounces oven-baked frozen French fries. Each serving contains 234 calories.

480 calories per serving

Colorful Beef Plate

2 servings

8 ounces beef brisket or bottom round

Salt

¼ bay leaf

1 small leek (4 ounces), cleaned and cut into julienne

1 carrot

2 ounces celery root, peeled and cut into julienne (⅔ cup)

1 small onion, cut into eighths

Preparation: 1½ hours

Each serving contains 302 calories, 19 g protein, 9 g carbohydrate, 19 g fat

Add beef to 3 cups boiling salted water. Add bay leaf, cover and cook for 1 hour. Add vegetables and cook another 20 minutes. Place meat on plates and

62

surround with vegetables. Spoon some of the broth over beef.

Accompaniments: Salad made of 2 small boiled potatoes (8 ounces), cubed and dressed with ½ cup plain yogurt and 1 egg yolk; also, one 16-ounce jar pickled beets, drained. Each serving contains 208 calories.

510 calories per serving

Grilled Kabob

2 servings

1 slice filet mignon (3½ ounces)

1 slice boneless pork loin (3½ ounces)

1 veal cutlet (3½ ounces)

1 small onion, peeled

1 medium-large zucchini (8 ounces), thickly sliced

2 to 4 large hot red peppers

2 small apples (4 ounces each), peeled, cored and cut into thick wedges

Salt and pepper

Garlic powder

2 teaspoons oil

Preparation: 30 minutes

**Each serving contains 316 calories,
31 g protein, 12 g carbohydrate, 13 g fat**

Halve meat slices and pat dry with paper towels. Preheat broiler. Thread meats, vegetables, peppers and apple wedges on two metal skewers. Mix salt, pepper and garlic powder with oil. Brush carefully onto kabobs. Grill, turning frequently, until done, about 20 minutes.

Accompaniments: ¼ cup raw long-grain rice, cooked and seasoned with paprika. Each serving contains 74 calories.

390 calories per serving

Hungarian Lecso

2 servings

2 strips lean bacon, chopped

1 cup chopped onion

2 teaspoons oil

4 ounces each lean, boneless beef and pork, cut into ¾-inch cubes

2 green peppers, cut into strips

⅓ cup chicken broth

1½ tablespoons raw rice

1 small tomato, peeled and chopped

Salt and pepper

1 tablespoon sweet paprika

Preparation: 50 minutes

**Each serving contains 310 calories,
23 g protein, 18 g carbohydrate, 13 g fat**

Fry bacon in Dutch oven. Add onion and sauté until golden brown. Add oil and heat. Add meat cubes and sauté 5 minutes, stirring. Remove meat from pan. Add pepper strips, broth and rice, cover and simmer 15 minutes. Add meat and chopped tomato and simmer 10 minutes. Season with salt, pepper and paprika.

Accompaniment: 5 tablespoons raw rice, cooked. Each serving contains 110 calories.

420 calories per serving

Almond Liver on Toast

2 servings

8 ounces calves' liver

1 tablespoon flour

2 teaspoons oil

Salt and pepper

1 teaspoon instant beef broth granules

¼ cup dry red wine

1 tablespoon raisins

2 tablespoons slivered almonds

63

Grilled Ham Rolls

California Steak

Hunter's Venison Stew

Summer Turkey Breast

Almond Liver on Toast

Mushroom Cream Cutlets

1 tablespoon chopped parsley

2 slices toast

Preparation: 25 minutes

Each serving contains 26 g protein, 26 g carbohydrate, 15 g fat

Cut liver into strips and dust with flour. Heat oil in skillet and sauté liver 2 minutes. Remove from pan and season with salt and pepper. Add broth, wine and raisins to pan and stir until boiling. Return liver to skillet and cook another 2 minutes. Stir in almonds and parsley. Serve on toast.

380 calories per serving

Delicate Potted Liver

2 servings

4 teaspoons margarine

8 ounces beef liver, cut into pieces

1 small red and 1 small green pepper, cut into strips

½ cup sliced onion

½ cup beef broth (made from bouillon cube)

¼ cup red wine

1 dill pickle, sliced

Salt and pepper

Garlic powder

1 teaspoon cornstarch

Half of one 11-ounce can mandarin oranges, drained (reserve liquid)

Preparation: 30 minutes

Each serving contains 372 calories, 30 g protein, 26 g carbohydrate, 14 g fat

Melt margarine in saucepan. Add liver, pepper strips and onion slices and stir-fry. Add broth, wine and add pickle slices, cover and simmer 15 minutes. Season with salt, pepper and garlic powder. Mix cornstarch with a little water and stir into sauce to thicken.

Stir in oranges and heat through. Thin sauce with a little of the mandarin orange juice if you wish.

Accompaniments: Salad of 1 head Boston lettuce dressed with 2 teaspoons each oil and vinegar; also, 2 portions mashed potatoes (1 cup per person). Each serving contains 168 calories.

540 calories per serving

Green Pea Soup With Sausages

2 servings

2 small boiling potatoes (8 ounces), peeled and diced

1 cup beef broth (made from bouillon cubes)

2 teaspoons margarine

¼ cup chopped onion

1 cup cooked green peas (with their cooking liquid)

8 ounces canned Vienna sausage, drained

1 tablespoon chopped parsley

½ cup grated Edam cheese

Salt and white pepper

Preparation: 20 minutes

Each serving contains 26 g protein, 38 g carbohydrate, 14 g fat

Add potatoes to broth, cover and simmer 15 minutes. Melt margarine in skillet, add onion and simmer 15 minutes. Melt margarine in skillet, add onion and sauté until golden brown. Add peas with cooking liquid and sausages to potatoes; heat for 5 minutes. Stir in parsley and cheese. Season with salt and pepper.

Tip: 1 cup peas and carrots or cut green beans can be used instead of 1 cup peas. With green beans, grated Parmesan cheese tastes especially good; since it is higher in calories than Edam cheese, use only ¼ cup.

450 calories per serving

Delicate Leek Toast

2 servings

1 large leek (8 ounces)

2 teaspoons butter or margarine

2 slices cooked canned ham (3½ ounces total), cut into thin strips

Salt

2 slices rye toast

2 ounces (½ cup) grated Edam cheese

Preparation: 20 minutes

Each serving contains 310 calories, 20 g protein, 18 g carbohydrate, 16 g fat

Preheat oven to 450°F. Clean leek thoroughly and cut into rings. Melt butter in saucepan. Sauté ham and leek 5 minutes. Salt lightly. Place toast on cookie sheet. Top first with ham mixture, then cheese. Bake until cheese is melted, about 8 minutes.

Accompaniment: Salad of 1 medium-size sliced cucumber with a dressing of vinegar, 1 tablespoon oil and 1 tablespoon chopped parsley. Each serving contains 60 calories.

370 calories per serving

Grilled Ham Rolls

2 servings

2 slices cooked ham (2 ounces each)

2 thin slices Edam cheese (1 ounce each)

1 cup sauerkraut

1 teaspoon caraway seed

2 slices sesame crispbread

1 cup tomato sauce, heated

Preparation: 15 minutes

Each serving contains 291 calories, 18 g protein, 17 g carbohydrate, 15 g fat

Heat grill. Top ham slices with cheese slices. Mix sauerkraut and caraway; place on cheese. Roll up

and secure with toothpicks. Grill 5 minutes, turning from time to time. (Rolls can also be placed in a skillet and cooked without fat for 10 minutes; cover skillet toward end of cooking time.) Serve rolls with crispbread and tomato sauce.

Accompaniment: 3 medium tomatoes, sliced and seasoned with salt and pepper. Each serving contains 29 calories.

320 calories per serving

Ham Cream Endive

2 servings

4 Belgian endive (1 pound)

Salt and curry powder

4 slices cooked canned ham (1½ ounces each)

2 teaspoons margarine

¼ cup cream

5 tablespoons evaporated milk

1 teaspoon cornstarch

1 teaspoon chopped chives

Preparation: 25 minutes

Each serving contains 350 calories, 21 g protein, 10 g carbohydrate, 22 g fat

Wash endive and cut out the bitter core. Bring 1 cup water to boil, adding some of salt and curry powder. Add endive, cover and cook 10 minutes. Drain. Roll a slice of ham around each endive. Melt margarine in a skillet and sauté rolls on all sides. Season cream and evaporated milk with salt and curry powder. Pour over endive rolls, cover and simmer 10 minutes. Transfer rolls to plates. Mix cornstarch with a little water to make thin paste. Add to pan juices and stir until thickened. Season sauce and pour over rolls. Sprinkle with chives.

Accompaniment: 2 small boiled potatoes (8 ounces). Each serving contains 85 calories.

Tip: Do not cook endive in an aluminum pot; it will turn the vegetable an unappetizing gray color.

435 calories per serving

67

Tournedos with Tomatoes

Paprika Steak

Pork Filet with Banana

Green Pea Soup
with Sausages

Quick Cauliflower Plate

Ham With Melon, Roman Style

2 servings

1 very small honeydew melon (1¼ to 1½ pounds)

1 orange, peeled and diced

1 cup chopped celery

2 teaspoons chopped pistachios

½ cup black grapes, halved and seeded

2 tablespoons grappa

Salt and white pepper

Ground ginger

6 ounces prosciutto

1 tablespoon mayonnaise

¼ cup sour cream

1 teaspoon mustard

1 teaspoon lemon juice

Pinch of cayenne pepper

Preparation: 30 minutes, without marinating time

Each serving contains 353 calories, 19 g protein, 23 g carbohydrate, 17 g fat

Halve melon by making zig-zag cuts for a decorative edge. Remove seeds from both halves. Scoop out melon flesh with a spoon; dice. Chill melon shells. Mix melon, orange, celery and grapes. Add grappa, salt, pepper and ginger and chill 1 hour. Spoon salad into melon halves. Roll up prosciutto and arrange next to melon. Mix mayonnaise, sour cream, mustard and lemon juice. Season with salt and cayenne. Spoon over salad.

Accompaniments: 2 slices toast spread with 1 tablespoon whipped margarine. Each serving contains 87 calories.

440 calories per serving

Pork Filet With Banana

2 servings

4 small pork filet steaks (2 ounces each)

Salt and pepper

Sweet paprika

2 teaspoons oil

¼ cup sliced onion

2 small bananas

1 tablespoon chopped parsley

Preparation: 15 minutes

Each serving contains 320 calories, 20 g protein, 23 g carbohydrate, 15 g fat

Pound steaks until thin and flat. Season with salt, pepper and paprika. Heat oil in skillet and brown steaks for 5 minutes on both sides, adding onion rings after 2 minutes. Add 2 tablespoons hot water. Meanwhile, peel bananas and halve lengthwise. Transfer steaks to heated platter and keep warm. Add bananas to pan juices and sauté 5 minutes. Dust with paprika. Add to steaks. Sprinkle with chopped parsley.

Accompaniments: 1 pound cooked asparagus with 1 teaspoon butter, salt and pepper; also, 1 cup canned baby peas heated with 1 teaspoon butter. Each serving contains 140 calories.

460 calories per serving

Mushroom Mustard Cutlet

2 servings

1 tablespoon red wine vinegar

2 teaspoons oil

Salt

Coarsely ground pepper

1 teaspoon mustard

2 pork cutlets (4 ounces each)

8 ounces fresh mushrooms, sliced

1 tablespoon chopped parsley

Preparation: 20 minutes, without marinating time

70

Each serving contains 282 calories, 29 g protein, 4 g carbohydrate, 15 g fat

Mix vinegar, 1 teaspoon oil, salt, pepper and mustard. Brush on pork cutlets. Marinate in bowl for 1 hour. Fry steaks in skillet for 5 minutes or until golden brown. Place on warmed plates. Add mushrooms to skillet. Season to taste and stir in parsley. Cook until tender and serve over pork.

Accompaniments: 6 ounces frozen peas (⅔ of one 10-ounce package), cooked according to package directions; 1 cup mashed potatoes (½ cup per person). Each serving contains 118 calories.

400 calories per serving

Quick Cauliflower Plate

2 servings

1 cauliflower (1¼ pounds)

Salt

Nutmeg

2 pork filet steaks (4 ounces each)

2 teaspoons oil

½ cup chopped onion

¼ cup grated Parmesan cheese

1½ cups hot prepared instant mashed potatoes (no butter)

Preparation: 25 minutes

Each serving contains 34 g protein, 33 g carbohydrate, 20 g fat

Clean cauliflower and separate into florets. Bring salted water to a boil. Add cauliflower and cook 20 minutes. Drain and season with salt and nutmeg. Flatten steaks lightly with hands. Heat oil in skillet and fry steaks 2½ minutes on each side. Transfer steaks to heated plate and keep warm. Sauté onion in pan drippings until golden brown. Add 2 tablespoons water and simmer 5 minutes. Place on meat. Add drained cauliflower. Sprinkle with cheese. Add potatoes to plates.

460 calories per serving

Garlic Veal Steak

2 servings

1 garlic clove

Salt

1 tablespoon oil

Coarsely ground black pepper

2 veal steaks (4 ounces each)

1 tablespoon chopped chives

Preparation: 10 minutes, without marinating time

Each serving contains 180 calories, 25 g protein, 0 g carbohydrate, 6 g fat

Peel garlic. Sprinkle with salt and crush with a fork in small bowl. Add oil and pepper and blend. Brush veal steaks with this mixture and let marinate in bowl 30 minutes. Preheat broiler. Place steaks on grill and broil 2 minutes on each side. Serve sprinkled with chives.

Accompaniments: Salad of 12 ounces cooked cut green beans, in a dressing of 2 tablespoons herb vinegar with herbs as desired and 2 teaspoons oil; 2 slices sesame crispbread. Each serving contains 130 calories.

310 calories per serving

Mushroom Cream Cutlets

2 servings

2 teaspoons oil

¼ cup chopped onion

2 veal cutlets (4 ounces each), cut into thin strips

Salt and white pepper

8 ounces fresh mushrooms, sliced

2 tablespoons white wine

1 tablespoon flour

7 tablespoons plain yogurt

5 tablespoons sour cream

71

Gourmet Stuffed Celery Root

Ham Cream Endive

Colorful Meat and Vegetables

Soy Leeks and Mushrooms

Gourmet Asparagus Fricassee

Greek Carrot Plaki

1 tablespoon chopped parsley

Sweet paprika

Preparation: 20 minutes

**Each serving contains 305 calories,
33 g protein, 12 g carbohydrate, 11 g fat**

Heat oil in skillet and sauté onion until golden. Add veal and cook 5 minutes. Season with salt and pepper. Add mushrooms and heat through. Add wine and cook 5 minutes. Whisk flour with yogurt and cream. Stir into pan and cook 3 minutes. Season with salt and pepper. Stir in chopped parsley. Transfer to bowl and dust with paprika..

Accompaniments: Salad of 1 medium cucumber, chopped, 1 large green pepper, chopped, and 1 medium-large tomato, peeled and chopped, dressed with 2 tablespoons lemon juice, herbs as desired, 2 tablespoons chopped parsley and 2 teaspoons oil. Also, ¼ cup raw long-grain rice, cooked. Each serving contains 175 calories.

480 calories per serving

Baked Veal Cutlet

2 servings

2 veal cutlets (4 ounces each)

1 teaspoon Worcestershire sauce

1 tablespoon lemon juice

Salt and white pepper

2 teaspoons oil

2 slices white bread (1 ounce each)

1 tablespoon catsup

2 plum tomatoes, sliced

1 tablespoon chopped parsley

3 thin slices Edam cheese (½ ounce each)

Sweet paprika

Preparation: 25 minutes

**Each serving contains 330 calories,
35 g protein, 16 g carbohydrate, 13 g fat**

Pound veal until thin. Sprinkle with Worcestershire sauce and lemon juice. Season with salt and pepper. Position rack in upper part of oven and preheat to 400°F. Heat oil in skillet and sauté veal 3 minutes on each side. Toast bread and place on 2 heatproof plates. Top with veal. Spread with catsup and top with tomato slices. Season with salt and pepper, and sprinkle with parsley. Halve cheese slices diagonally. Arrange 3 triangles on each piece of veal. Place on upper shelf in oven. Bake 10 to 15 minutes. Sprinkle with paprika before serving.

Accompaniment: Salad of 4 ounces leaf lettuce and ⅓ cup sliced onion, with a dressing of vinegar, herbs as desired and 2 teaspoons oil. Each serving contains 60 calories.

390 calories per serving

Colorful Meat and Vegetables

2 servings

8 ounces veal scaloppine, diced

Salt and white pepper

4 teaspoons margarine

1 tablespoon soy flour

1 cup hot chicken broth (made from bouillon cubes)

6 ounces frozen peas (⅔ of one 10-ounce package)

¼ cup grated cucumber

One 8½-ounce can corn, partially drained

Preparation: 25 minutes

**Each serving contains 39 g protein,
25 g carbohydrate, 12 g fat**

Season veal with salt and pepper. Melt margarine in skillet and sauté veal 5 minutes. Dust with soy flour and sauté for another 3 minutes. Slowly add hot broth, stirring constantly. Add frozen peas and grated cucumber and simmer 15 minutes. Add corn with some of the juices in can; heat through. Taste and adjust seasoning.

410 calories per serving

74

Veal Ragout With Peas

2 servings

8 ounces veal shoulder, cut into ¾-inch cubes

1 small leek (4 ounces), coarsely chopped

1 medium carrot, coarsely chopped

Salt

1 very small onion, halved

6 ounces frozen peas

2 teaspoons butter or margarine

1 tablespoon flour

Tabasco

Preparation: 50 minutes

**Each serving contains 280 calories,
32 g protein, 19 g carbohydrate, 6 g fat**

Combine veal, leek and carrot in saucepan. Season with salt and add water to cover by the thickness of a finger. Cover and cook over medium heat 30 minutes. Brown cut surface of onion halves in hot skillet; add to meat. Cook peas in small amount of salted water for 8 minutes or until tender; drain. Melt butter or margarine in saucepan. Whisk in flour. Slowly add broth strained from veal, whisking constantly until sauce thickens. Stir in veal, vegetables and peas. Season with salt and Tabasco.

Accompaniment: 5 tablespoons raw rice, cooked. Each serving contains 110 calories.

390 calories per serving

Tunisian Lamb Ragout

2 servings

2 teaspoons oil

8 ounces lean lamb, cut into small cubes

Salt

¼ cup dry red wine

Peel of 1 orange

2 medium tomatoes, peeled and quartered

1 garlic clove, finely chopped

1 cup chopped onion

2 tablespoons orange juice

White pepper

Large pinch of cinnamon

Pinch of cayenne pepper

Preparation: 50 minutes

**Each serving contains 282 calories,
25 g protein, 9 g carbohydrate, 13 g fat**

Heat oil in saucepan over medium-high heat. Add lamb cubes and brown on all sides. Season with salt. Add wine and orange peel and bring to boil. Stir in tomato, garlic and onion, cover and simmer 40 minutes. Pour in orange juice. Season ragout with white pepper, cinnamon and cayenne. If mixture is too liquid, simmer until juices thicken.

Accompaniment: 2 ounces spaghetti, cooked in boiling salted water, drained and tossed with 2 tablespoons grated Parmesan cheese. Each serving contains 158 calories.

440 calories per serving

Garden Turkey Salad

2 servings

8 ounces cooked turkey meat, diced

Salt and white pepper

Garlic powder

4 teaspoons oil

4 ounces mushrooms, thinly sliced

1 tablespoon lemon juice

8 ounces small spinach leaves

½ cup chopped onion

1 bunch radishes, sliced

2 tablespoons wine vinegar

Pinch each of dried tarragon, rosemary, chervil and sage

75

Delicate Potted Liver

Tunisian Lamb Ragout

Colorful Beef Plate

Veal Ragout with Peas

Tarragon Chicken

Hungarian Lecso

Preparation: 25 minutes

**Each serving contains 265 calories,
28 g protein, 8 g carbohydrate, 11 g fat**

Season turkey with salt, pepper and garlic powder. Heat 1 tablespoon oil in skillet and sauté turkey 2 minutes; cool. Sprinkle mushrooms with lemon juice in bowl. Add spinach, onion and radishes. Make a dressing of wine vinegar, crumbled herbs, salt, pepper and remaining 1 teaspoon oil. Spoon over salad.

Accompaniments: 2 slices whole-grain rye bread (1½ ounces each) spread with 1 tablespoon whipped butter. Each serving contains 115 calories.

Tip: If you would like more dressing, add a little instant broth mixed with water.

380 calories per serving

Summery Turkey Breast

2 servings

2 slices turkey breast (4 ounces each)

Salt and white pepper

Curry powder

4 teaspoons oil

1 package (10 ounces) frozen mixed vegetables

2 teaspoons margarine

1 tablespoon chopped parsley

Parsley and dill sprigs for garnish

Preparation: 30 minutes

**Each serving contains 330 calories,
34 g protein, 10 g carbohydrate, 15 g fat**

Season turkey with salt and white pepper. Dust lightly with curry powder. Heat oil in deep skillet and sauté turkey over medium-high heat 5 minutes on each side. Reduce heat to low and cook another 3 minutes on each side. Transfer turkey to heated platter and keep warm. Place unthawed vegetables in pan. Add 2 tablespoons water and margarine. Season with salt and pepper, cover and steam 15 minutes. Stir in chopped parsley. Place vegetables in a warmed

bowl and top with turkey. Garnish with parsley and dill.

Accompaniment: 8 ounces oven-baked frozen French fries. Each serving contains 128 calories.

460 calories per serving

Tarragon Chicken

2 servings

1 small broiler-fryer (about 1½ pounds)

1 small bunch tarragon

1 small bunch parsley

Salt

⅓ cup grated onion

1 teaspoon sweet paprika

¼ cup evaporated milk

1 tablespoon flour

2 teaspoons oil

Preparation: 50 minutes

**Each serving contains 388 calories,
41 g protein, 9 g carbohydrate, 17 g fat**

Preheat oven to 350°F. or prepare grill. Wash chicken inside and out; pat dry. Trim tarragon and parsley, tie into a bunch and place inside chicken. Close opening with toothpicks. Rub chicken lightly with salt. Combine onion, paprika, evaporated milk, flour and oil to form a paste; brush chicken with mixture. Roast in oven or grill on a spit for 40 minutes. Cut chicken in half, discard herbs and place chicken on plates.

Accompaniments: Salad of 1 medium-size sliced cucumber and 1 small sliced tomato dressed with vinegar, desired herbs and 1 tablespoon chopped parsley (no oil). Also, ¼ cup raw rice, cooked until tender. Each serving contains 92 calories.

480 calories per serving

Gourmet Asparagus Fricassee

2 servings

2 boiling onions

1 whole clove

½ bay leaf

Salt

2 boned, skinned chicken breast halves (8 ounces)

3½ ounces lean ground beef

2 tablespoons cream

1 tablespoon dry breadcrumbs

White pepper

1 tablespoon flour

1 can (4 ounces) sliced mushrooms, drained

1 can (10½ ounces) asparagus, drained

Grated peel of 1 orange

1 tablespoon orange juice

1 egg yolk

Preparation: 1 hour

**Each serving contains 367 calories,
46 g protein, 14 g carbohydrate, 11 g fat**

Peel onions. Press clove and bay leaf into one of the onions. Place this onion and 1½ cups water in saucepan and bring to boil. Sprinkle in salt. Add chicken breasts and simmer 20 minutes. Finely chop the second onion and mix with ground beef, cream, breadcrumbs, salt and pepper. Shape into small balls, add to saucepan and simmer 5 minutes. Remove chicken and meatballs. Cut chicken into pieces; strain broth into another saucepan. Mix flour with a little water. Stir into broth and heat until thickened. Add mushrooms, asparagus, chicken, meatballs, orange peel and juice, salt and pepper. Beat some of the hot sauce into the egg yolk, then return mixture to remaining sauce and blend well. Heat through but do not boil.

Accompaniment: ¼ cup raw rice, cooked with 3½ ounces (⅓ of a 10-ounce package) frozen peas. Each serving contains 103 calories.

470 calories per serving

Hunter's Venison Stew

2 servings

4 teaspoons margarine

12 ounces venison meat, cut into 1-inch cubes

½ cup chopped onion

1 garlic clove, mashed

2 juniper berries

2 medium tomatoes, peeled and quartered

¼ cup dry red wine

Salt

1 tablespoon brandy or Cognac

1 can (4 ounces) sliced mushrooms

1 teaspoon cornstarch

½ cup plain yogurt

Pinch of cayenne pepper

Preparation: 1 hour

**Each serving contains 363 calories,
36 g protein, 13 g carbohydrate, 13 g fat**

Melt margarine in Dutch oven and brown venison cubes on all sides. Add onion, garlic and juniper berries and sauté briefly. Add tomatoes and wine, season with salt, cover and simmer until meat is tender, about 40 to 50 minutes. Add brandy and mushrooms. Whisk cornstarch into yogurt and stir into stew to thicken. Heat until bubbling and season with cayenne.

Accompaniment: 2 servings (¾ cup each) mashed potatoes (no butter). Each serving contains 107 calories.

470 calories per serving

Colorful Tuna Salad

2 servings

1 small can (3¼ ounces) tuna packed in oil, drained (reserve 2 teaspoons oil)

6 Boston lettuce leaves

79

Flamed Pepper Steak

Summer Salad Tobias

Delicate Asparagus Omelet
with Shrimp

Cheese-Stuffed Pepper Rings

Colorful Tuna Salad

Grilled Kabob

2 small tomatoes, peeled and sliced

1 medium cucumber, sliced

2 hard-cooked eggs, sliced

½ cup thinly sliced onion, separated into rings

Salt

Marinade:

3 tablespoons herb vinegar

1 tablespoon soy sauce

1 teaspoon chopped capers

2 teaspoons oil drained from tuna

2 teaspoons soy oil

Salt and white pepper

Preparation: 20 minutes

**Each serving contains 346 calories,
20 g protein, 7 g carbohydrate, 24 g fat**

Flake tuna and place on center of platter. Arrange vegetables and egg slices in groups around tuna. Top tuna with onion rings. Lightly salt tomato and cucumber slices.

Whisk marinade ingredients together, adding salt and pepper to taste. Spoon over salad.

Accompaniments: 4 slices whole-wheat crispbread spread with 4 teaspoons whipped butter or margarine. Each serving contains 114 calories.

460 calories per serving

Smoked Salmon Salad

2 servings

6 ounces frozen peas (⅔ of one 10-ounce package)

Salt

6 Boston lettuce leaves

6 ounces sliced smoked salmon

2 plum tomatoes, peeled and sliced

1 small cucumber, sliced

1 hard-cooked egg

2 lemon wedges

2 teaspoons soy oil

2 tablespoons dill vinegar

Salt and white pepper

Dill sprigs for garnish

Preparation: 30 minutes, without marinating time

**Each serving contains 328 calories,
26 g protein, 14 g carbohydrate, 18 g fat**

Cook peas according to package directions. Drain and cool. Place lettuce leaves on two plates and top with smoked salmon. Place tomato and cucumber slices on plates along with peas. Cut egg into eighths and divide between plates. Add lemon wedges. Mix soy oil, dill vinegar, salt and pepper. Sprinkle over salad. Garnish with dill sprigs.

Accompaniment: 4 thin slices melba toast (½ ounce each). Each serving contains 52 calories.

Tip: This salad can also be made with smoked sturgeon; 6 ounces contains 33 fewer calories than smoked salmon.

380 calories per serving

Summer Salad Tobias

2 servings

1 small head Boston lettuce

1 medium-size red and 1 medium-size green pepper, seeded and cut into strips

1 tart apple (6 ounces), peeled, cored and cut into wedges

1 orange (6 ounces), peeled and sectioned

1 grapefruit (8 ounces), peeled and sectioned

2 plum tomatoes, peeled and diced

3½ ounces cooked, shelled and deveined shrimp

1 tablespoon lemon juice

82

1 tablespoon mayonnaise

½ cup plain yogurt

Salt and white pepper

1 teaspoon curry powder

Preparation: 30 minutes

Each serving contains 269 calories, 16 g protein, 35 g carbohydrate, 6 g fat

Wash lettuce and tear leaves into bite-size pieces. Combine lettuce, peppers, apple wedges, orange and grapefruit sections, tomatoes, shrimp and lemon juice. Mix mayonnaise with yogurt. Season to taste with salt, pepper and curry powder. Spoon onto salad.

Accompaniments: 2 slices whole-grain wheat bread (1 ounce each) spread with 2 teaspoons whipped butter. Each serving contains 91 calories.

Tip: If you like, eat this with a broiled lean filet mignon weighing 4 ounces. This will add 158 calories to each serving.

360 calories per serving

Shrimp Japanese Style

2 servings

12 ounces frozen shrimp, thawed

½ small leek (2 ounces)

4 teaspoons oil

6 ounces frozen peas (²/₃ of one 10-ounce package)

2 tablespoons soy sauce

Salt and white pepper

Preparation: 25 minutes

Each serving contains 263 calories, 25 g protein, 11 g carbohydrate, 12 g fat

Drain shrimp and pat dry with paper towels. Trim leek and cut into thin rings. Wash thoroughly. Heat oil in skillet, add shrimp and stir constantly until lightly browned. Add leek and sauté until golden. Add frozen peas, cover and simmer 6 minutes. Stir in soy sauce. If necessary, season with salt and pepper.

Accompaniment: ¼ cup raw rice, cooked and mixed with 1 tablespoon soy sauce. Each serving contains 77 calories.

Tip: Try substituting lobster meat for shrimp if you can find it in your supermarket. The difference in calories is negligible: 6 ounces lobster meat contains 160 calories, 6 ounces shrimp about 151.

340 calories per serving

Holiday Trout

2 servings

4 ounces frozen shrimp, thawed

2 whole trout (8 ounces each), cleaned

2 tablespoons lemon juice

Salt and white pepper

2 tablespoons flour

4 teaspoons oil

1 tablespoon chopped almonds

5 tablespoons sour cream

Preparation: 30 minutes

Each serving contains 392 calories, 38 g protein, 9 g carbohydrate, 20 g fat

Sprinkle shrimp and trout with lemon juice. Season with salt and pepper and roll in flour. Heat oil in skillet and sauté trout 5 minutes on each side. Add shrimp and almonds and cook 5 minutes; remove from pan and keep warm. Stir sour cream into pan juices. Season to taste and spoon over trout.

Accompaniment: 2 small boiled potatoes (8 ounces). Each serving contains 88 calories.

480 calories per serving

Provençal Fish Filets

2 servings

2 haddock filets (8 ounces each)

1 tablespoon lemon juice

Oil

83

Florentine Haddock

Holiday Trout

Fisherman's Sunday Ragout

Italian Fish Slices

Shrimp Japanese Style

Provençal Fish Fillets

¾ cup sliced onion

1 garlic clove, chopped

1 large green pepper, seeded and cut into strips

2 medium tomatoes, peeled and diced

10 stuffed green olives, sliced

1 teaspoon sweet paprika

2 teaspoons Herbes de Provence or fines herbes

Salt and pepper

1 tablespoon flour

Preparation: 35 minutes

**Each serving contains 365 calories,
40 g protein, 16 g carbohydrate, 13 g fat**

Sprinkle fish with lemon juice and let marinate. Preheat broiler. Heat 4 teaspoons oil in skillet and sauté onion slices and garlic until golden brown. Add pepper strips and tomato and sauté 15 minutes. Add olive slices, paprika, herbs, salt and pepper. Taste and adjust seasoning. Lightly oil broiler rack. Pat filets dry and brush lightly on both sides with oil. Dust filets with flour and broil 5 minutes on each side. Season with salt and pepper and serve with vegetables on a warmed platter.

Accompaniment: 2 slices whole-grain wheat bread. Each serving contains 75 calories.

440 calories per serving

Italian Fish Slices

2 servings

4 codfish filets (4 ounces each)

2 tablespoons lemon juice

¾ cup thinly sliced onion

2 plum tomatoes, peeled and sliced

Salt

Pinch of dried thyme

2 slices (1 ounce each) Edam cheese

Lemon wedges for garnish

Preparation: 45 minutes

**Each serving contains 289 calories,
31 g protein, 6 g carbohydrate, 13 g fat**

Rinse filets and pat dry. Sprinkle with lemon juice and let stand to marinate. Preheat oven to 400°F. Season filets with salt. Place 2 in ovenproof pan; top with onion rings and tomato slices. Sprinkle with thyme. Arrange cheese slices on top; do not let them extend over edges of filets. Top with remaining fish. Cover pan with foil and bake 25 minutes. Remove foil and garnish with lemon wedges.

Accompaniments: Half of a 10-ounce package frozen Italian or mixed vegetables, cooked according to package directions; stir in 1 teaspoon margarine. Also, ¼ cup raw long-grain rice, cooked and mixed with 1 teaspoon chopped parsley. Each serving contains 191 calories.

480 calories per serving

Florentine Haddock

2 servings

2 haddock filets (8 ounces each)

1 tablespoon lemon juice

1 pound fresh spinach, stemmed

2 teaspoons oil

½ cup coarsely chopped onion

Salt and white pepper

Garlic powder

1 teaspoon margarine

Nutmeg

2 plum tomatoes, peeled and sliced

Onion powder

1 ounce Edam cheese, coarsely shredded (¼ cup)

Preparation: 50 minutes

**Each serving contains 335 calories,
45 g protein, 10 g carbohydrate, 9 g fat**

86

Rinse fish in cold water, pat dry and sprinkle with lemon juice. Wash spinach, drain and tear into large pieces. Heat oil in skillet and sauté onion until golden brown. Push onion to one side of skillet, add fish filets and sauté 3 minutes per side. Season with salt, pepper and garlic powder. Position rack to center of oven and preheat to 400°F. Melt margarine in oven-proof pan. Add spinach, cover and simmer 3 minutes. Season with salt, pepper and nutmeg. Remove from heat and top with fish filets. Arrange tomato slices over fish. Season with salt and onion powder. Sprinkle with cheese. Bake 15 minutes.

Accompaniment: 2 portions mashed potatoes (1 cup per person). Each serving contains 105 calories.

440 calories per serving

Fisherman's Sunday Ragout

2 servings

12 ounces red snapper filets, cut into pieces

1 tablespoon lemon juice

Pepper

Garlic powder

1 teaspoon instant chicken broth granules

1 tablespoon oil

3 tablespoons chopped parsley

1 large leek (8 ounces)

2 teaspoons margarine

½ cup chopped onion

1 teaspoon flour

½ cup chicken broth (made from bouillon cube)

½ cup milk

1 can (4 ounces) sliced mushrooms, drained

½ red pepper, seeded and diced

1 egg yolk

2 tablespoons sour cream

Preparation: 1 hour

Each serving contains 426 calories, 37 g protein, 21 g carbohydrate, 17 g fat

Toss fish pieces with lemon juice. Mix some pepper, garlic powder and broth granules with oil and parsley. Stir in fish and marinate 20 minutes. Trim leek, cut into rings and wash. Melt margarine in skillet and sauté leek and onion until golden brown. Dust with flour and sauté until flour is golden. Add broth and milk and stir until thickened. Stir in mushroom slices, diced pepper and fish; cover and simmer 7 minutes. Whisk egg yolk with sour cream. Stir in some of the hot sauce, then return mixture to skillet and heat but do not boil. Season to taste.

Accompaniment: ¼ cup raw long-grain rice, cooked. Each serving contains 74 calories.

500 calories per serving

87

Desserts—Lower in Calories

Getting thin should enhance your frame of mind, not spoil it. With this in mind, what follows are a few desserts (or between-meal snacks) that contain between 68 and 152 calories a portion. Though they contain no sugar, they are sweet rewards for a dedicated dieter. Figure these sugarless desserts into your daily calorie intake whenever you wish.

Baked Cheese

6 servings

1 pound farmer cheese

2 eggs

Pinch of salt

Pinch each of cinnamon and cloves

⅓ cup lemon juice

Liquid non-caloric sweetener

Preparation: 1 hour 10 minutes, plus resting time

**Each piece contains 106 calories,
17 g protein, 3 g carbohydrate, 3 g fat**

Line a sieve with cheesecloth. Add cheese, cover with cloth and let drain overnight in refrigerator. The next day press cheese through sieve into bowl. Add eggs and beat until smooth. Add salt, cinnamon, cloves and lemon juice. Stir in sweetener to taste. Position rack in center of oven and preheat to 400°F. Line bottom of 8-inch square pan with foil. Add cheese and spread into even layer. Bake 40 to 45 minutes. Cool cheese in pan, then chill overnight. Cut into 6 pieces.

Tip: This cheese can be refrigerated several days if wrapped in foil; don't be concerned if it weeps a little. Accompany baked cheese with 1 tablespoon low-calorie cherry preserves.

106 calories per serving

Strawberry Cheese

2 servings

1 pound strawberries

Liquid non-caloric sweetener

6 ounces (¾ cup) farmer cheese

3 tablespoons milk

Seeds scraped from ½ vanilla bean

Pinch of salt

2 fresh mint leaves

Preparation: 20 minutes

**Each serving contains 152 calories,
15 g protein, 18 g carbohydrate, 1 g fat**

Rinse berries with cold water, drain and hull. Halve strawberries. Place in bowl and add liquid sweetener to taste. Mix cheese with milk, vanilla and salt. Add liquid sweetener to taste. Divide cheese between 2 glasses. Top with berries and garnish with mint leaves.

Tip: You can also prepare this low-calorie but protein-rich cheese dessert with 1 pound raspberries, 8 ounces blackberries, 2 cups shredded apples, 2 cups diced orange, 1½ cups diced pears or 1 medium banana. All contain about the same number of calories but provide variety. Apples, pears and bananas should be sprinkled with lemon juice to prevent discoloration.

152 calories per serving

Coffee Gelatin With Cream

2 servings

2 teaspoons unflavored gelatin

Liquid non-caloric sweetener

1 cinnamon stick

1 piece of orange peel

1 tablespoon instant coffee, or more to taste

2 tablespoons rum

¼ cup heavy cream, whipped to soft peaks

Preparation: 20 minutes, without chilling

**Each serving contains 108 calories,
3 g protein, 1 g carbohydrate, 8 g fat**

Mix gelatin and 1 cup water in saucepan and let stand until gelatin is softened, about 5 minutes. Add sweetener, cinnamon stick and orange peel and place over low heat until gelatin dissolves, about 5 minutes. Remove cinnamon stick and orange peel. Stir in instant coffee and rum. Pour into 2 individual molds and chill until firm, about 2 hours. Dip molds into lukewarm water for a few seconds. Tap to loosen and unmold. Spoon whipped cream over gelatin.

Variation: For tea gelatin, which tastes tangier, bring 1 cup water to a boil, remove from heat and add 2 heaping teaspoons loose tea. Let steep 4 minutes (no longer, or it will be bitter). Substitute the tea for the water in recipe; omit coffee.

108 calories per serving

Pears in Gelatin

2 servings

2 medium-size juicy pears

2 tablespoons lemon juice

Pinch of cinnamon

Liquid non-caloric sweetener

2 teaspoons unflavored gelatin

½ cup dry white wine

1 scant cup (4 ounces) raspberries

Preparation: 30 minutes, without chilling

**Each serving contains 140 calories,
4 g protein, 19 g carbohydrate, 0 g fat**

Peel pears, leaving stem intact. Turn pears upside down and carefully remove cores. Bring 1 cup water to boil. Add pears, lemon juice and cinnamon; sweeten to taste with liquid sweetener. Cook for 10 minutes. Drain pears, reserving ½ cup syrup. Place reserved syrup in another saucepan and stir in gelatin. Let stand until gelatin is softened, about 5 minutes, then stir over low heat until gelatin is dissolved. Stir in white wine. Chill until syrupy. Divide gelatin mixture between 2 large glasses. Place pear into gelatin and chill until firm. Garnish with raspberries.

Tip: Try this using red wine instead of white; it makes the dessert more colorful. Garnish with

89

Baked Cheese

Strawberry Cheese

Coffee Gelatin with Cream

Pears in Gelatin

Whipped Yogurt

1 tablespoon whipped cream if you can afford the extra 45 calories.

140 calories per serving

Whipped Yogurt

2 servings

½ cup plain yogurt

1 tablespoon lemon juice

3 tablespoons dry red wine

Pinch of cinnamon

Liquid non-caloric sweetener

2 teaspoons unflavored gelatin

Few drops red food coloring

2 egg whites

Pinch of salt

2 fresh or maraschino cherries (with stems if possible)

Preparation: 25 minutes, without chilling

Each serving contains 68 calories, 9 g protein, 5 g carbohydrate, 0 g fat

Combine yogurt, lemon juice and wine and whisk until foamy. Add cinnamon and liquid sweetener to taste. Stir gelatin into ½ cup water. Add 1 to 2 drops red food coloring and let stand until gelatin is softened, about 5 minutes. Stir over low heat until gelatin is dissolved. Stir gelatin mixture into yogurt. Cover and chill just until slightly thickened. Beat egg whites with salt until stiff. Fold into yogurt mixture. Pour into two sherbet glasses and chill until firm. Garnish with cherries.

68 calories per serving

100-Calorie Snacks

Perhaps you want to reduce as fast as you can. Or on the other hand, maybe you're not in a big hurry, and would like to be able to snack now and then. In either case, here is an extensive list of 100-calorie snacks. They can be eaten instead of the between-meal foods morning and afternoon, saving about 100 calories per day. In 30 days this would amount to a savings of 3000 calories.

The foods are grouped in alphabetical order. You will have no problem finding something that appeals. Calorie calculations are based on edible weight: meat without bones, fruit without peel or seeds, cleaned vegetables, fish without bones and sausage and ham trimmed of visible fat. *Bon appetit!*

Baked Goods

Bran muffin	1½ ounces
Breadsticks, regular	2½
Corn muffin	1 ounce
English muffin	⅔ of a muffin
Gluten bread	3 slices
Melba toast	5 pieces
Pretzels	5
Pumpernickel	1½ slices
Ritz crackers	5
Rye Bread	1½ slices
Rye crisp or flatbread	4 double wafers
Saltine crackers	8
Social tea biscuits	5
White bread or toast	1½ slices
Wholewheat bread	1½ slices
Zwieback	3 pieces

Meat, Chicken, Sausage, Fish

Beef filet	2 ounces
Bologna	1 ounce
Caviar	1¼ ounces
Cervelat, soft	1 ounce
Chicken	2½ ounces
Corned beef	1 ounce
Crabmeat	3 ounces
Frankfurters with cereal filler	1
Ham	2 ounces
Hamburger, broiled	1½ ounces

Herring, pickled	2 ounces
Liver, beef	1½ ounces
Liverwurst	1 ounce
Roast beef, round	2 ounces
Roast pork	1½ ounces
Salmon, fresh	2 ounces
Salmon, smoked	2 ounces
Sardines in oil	2 ounces
Shrimp	4 ounces
Tongue	1½ ounces
Tuna, canned in water	3 ounces
Turkey, light meat	2 ounces
Veal cutlet	1½ ounces

Vegetables, Chips and Nuts

Almonds	13 to 15
Artichoke hearts, cooked	25 to 30
Asparagus, cooked	3 cups
Beets, cooked and sliced	2 cups
Brazil nuts	4 small
Carrots, cooked and diced	1½ cups
Cashews	8 large
Cauliflower, cooked	4½ cups
Celery, diced	5 cups
Corn on the cob, cooked	1 large ear
Green pepper, chopped	2½ cups
Hazelnuts	½ ounce
Olives, black	20 small
Olives, stuffed	20 extra large
Peanut butter	1 tablespoon
Peanuts	2 tablespoons
Pecans, chopped	2 tablespoons
Popcorn, popped	2 cups
Potato chips	10 two-inch chips
Sauerkraut, drained	3 cups
Sunflower seeds	½ ounce
Tomatoes	3 medium
Walnuts	2 tablespoons, chopped

Eggs, Cheese and Dairy Products

Buttermilk	1 cup
Skim milk	1¼ cups

Whole milk	⅔ cup
American cheese	1 ounce
Bleu cheese	1 ounce
Camembert	1¼ ounces
Cheese spread, American	2 tablespoons
Cottage cheese, skim milk	½ cup
Cream cheese	1 ounce
Edam cheese	1 ounce
Farmer cheese	⅓ cup
Gouda cheese	Scant 1 ounce
Swiss cheese	1 ounce
Yogurt, flavored (strawberry)	⅓ cup
Yogurt, plain (skim milk)	¾ cup
Egg, 1 large	80 calories

Fruit

Apple, fresh	1 large
Apple, dried	⅓ cup
Applesauce, unsweetened	1 cup
Apricots, dried	7 halves
Apricots, fresh	1¼ cups halves
Bananas	1 medium
Blueberries	1¼ cups
Cherries, Bing	1 cup pitted
Cherries, sour	8 ounces
Dates	3
Figs, canned	½ cup
Figs, dried	2 small
Figs, fresh	3
Grapefruit	1 medium
Grapes, fresh	1½ cups
Mandarin oranges	1¼ cups
Melon, cantaloupe, diced	2 cups
Melon, honeydew	2 cups
Melon, watermelon	2 cups
Orange, sections	¾ cup
Pears	1 medium
Pineapple, canned in pineapple juice	4 slices
Pineapple, fresh	2¼ cups
Plums, purple	¾ cup halves
Prunes	10 small
Raspberries, fresh	1 cup
Strawberries, fresh	2 cups

How to Slim Without Cooking

You can stick to your diet, even when you don't feel like cooking, by using carefully chosen prepared products. There is no loss of nutrients—just the advantage of not having to cook! The only thing you will need is hot water, and the menus provide around 1500 calories a day. If, for example, you normally have 2500 calories, you will lose three to four pounds in five days.

First Day (1 serving)

Breakfast

1 cup tomato juice (with herbs or spices, if desired)
2 slices whole-grain rye bread
2 teaspoons whipped butter or margarine
1 ounce low-fat Cheddar cheese
1 plum tomato, sliced and seasoned with salt and pepper

Coffee or tea
375 calories

Mid-morning

1 slice crispbread
1 teaspoon whipped butter or margarine
½ cup skim milk cottage cheese with herbs
1 dill pickle
150 calories

Lunch

1 cup canned tomato soup
Half a 1½-pound purchased broiled chicken
1 medium tomato, sliced and seasoned with onion salt and pepper

1 slice whole-grain wheat bread (1 ounce)

Tea, coffee or mineral water

435 calories

Afternoon

1 cup yogurt with fruit

1 slice crispbread

155 calories

Supper

1 slice crispbread

1 slice whole-grain wheat bread (1 ounce)

2 teaspoons whipped butter or margarine

2 ounces sliced smoked salmon

1½ ounces Camembert

1 medium apple

Tea, mineral water or low-calorie lemonade

375 calories

Total for the day: 118 g protein, 160 g carbohydrate, 32 g fat 1490 calories

Second Day (1 serving)

Breakfast

1 slice whole-grain wheat bread (1 ounce)

1 slice crispbread

2 teaspoons whipped butter or margarine

1 ounce ham

1 cooked egg

½ cup skim milk, hot or cold

Tea or coffee

375 calories

Mid-morning

1 slice crispbread

1 teaspoon whipped butter or margarine

1 ounce Camembert

1 dill pickle

150 calories

Lunch

1 cup instant broth, with 1 tablespoon grated Parmesan cheese stirred in

8 ounces cooked cod or other packaged unbreaded fish filets

1 slice whole-grain wheat bread (1 ounce)

Coffee, tea, mineral water or low-calorie lemonade

455 calories

Afternoon

1 slice crispbread

1 teaspoon whipped butter or margarine

1 large apple

160 calories

Supper

1 cup skim milk, hot or cold

2 slices whole-grain wheat bread (1 ounce each)

2 teaspoons whipped butter or margarine

1 ounce liverwurst

Tea, coffee or mineral water

355 calories

Total for day: 99 g protein, 127 g carbohydrate, 57 g fat 1495 calories

Third Day (1 serving)

Breakfast

½ cup skim milk

1 slice whole-grain rye bread

1 slice crispbread

2 teaspoons whipped butter or margarine

2 ounces canned or boiled ham

⅛ ounce of a honeydew melon

328 calories

Mid-morning

1 slice crispbread

1 teaspoon whipped butter or margarine

1 ounce canned or boiled ham

⅙ of a honeydew melon

153 calories

Lunch

2 slices lean corned beef (6 ounces)

1 slice whole-grain rye bread

2 teaspoons whipped butter or margarine

1 large green or red pepper, cut into strips

2 ounces (¼ cup) farmer cheese, mixed with a little water until creamy and flavored with liquid non-caloric sweetener and instant coffee (for dessert)

Coffee or tea

450 calories

Afternoon

1 slice crispbread

1 teaspoon whipped butter or margarine

1½ ounces canned or boiled ham

½ small green or red pepper

147 calories

Supper

1 cup bouillon (made from cubes)

2 slices whole-grain rye bread

2 ounces Camembert

1½ ounces hard cheese

Several slices of onion

Coffee, tea or mineral water

382 calories

Total for day: 115 g protein, 136 g carbohydrate, 45 g fat 1460 calories

Fourth Day (1 serving)

Breakfast

½ cup cranberry juice

1 slice whole-grain wheat bread

1 slice crispbread

2 teaspoons whipped butter or margarine

2 ounces mortadella or bologna

1 ounce Edam cheese

Tea or coffee

370 calories

Mid-morning

1 slice whole-grain wheat bread

1 teaspoon whipped butter or margarine

1 ounce mortadella or bologna

1 large dill pickle

150 calories

Lunch

1 cup bouillon, made from cubes and beaten with 1 egg yolk

4 ounces cooked pork

½ medium cucumber, sliced and seasoned with salt and pepper

½ cup plain yogurt

460 calories

Afternoon

1 slice crispbread

1 teaspoon whipped butter or margarine

1 large apple

160 calories

Supper

⅛ of a chilled large honeydew melon (12 ounces) with 2 ounces prosciutto, dusted with pepper

2 slices toast with 2 teaspoons butter

Coffee or tea

360 calories

Total for day: 83 g protein, 139 g carbohydrate, 66 g fat 1500 calories

100

Fifth Day (1 serving)

Breakfast

1 small orange

2 slices crispbread

2 teaspoons whipped butter or margarine

½ cup cottage cheese

2 ounces lean corned beef

1 plum tomato, sliced and seasoned with salt and pepper

Coffee or tea

379 calories

Mid-morning

1 slice crispbread

1 teaspoon whipped butter or margarine

1 ounce Edam cheese

155 calories

Lunch

1 cup mushroom soup

1 frankfurter

Mustard

2 slices whole-grain wheat bread

2 teaspoons whipped butter or margarine

1 medium tomato, sliced and seasoned with onion salt and pepper

450 calories

Afternoon

1 slice crispbread

1 teaspoon whipped butter or margarine

¾ cup plain yogurt

134 calories

Supper

*4 ounces (½ cup) farmer cheese, mixed with
2 tablespoons milk and 4 ounces cooked
shrimp, seasoned with salt and curry powder*

2 slices whole-grain wheat bread

2 teaspoons whipped butter or margarine

382 calories

Total for day: 105 g protein, 130 g carbohydrate,
51 g fat 1500 calories

15 Weekend Diets

When your waistband starts feeling tight and you can no longer deny that you've put on a few extra pounds, you may want to try a weekend diet. These are also good preventive diets—they will help you maintain weight loss even if your discipline slips a little during the week.

Apple Diet

A very strenuous diet, only for the completely healthy. For two days, eat a total of 6 unpeeled apples. With them drink as much fruit or herb tea as desired.

Weight loss: 3 to 5 pounds.

Apple-Egg Diet

If the Apple Diet is too rigorous, you can supplement each apple with a hard-cooked egg. For beverages, allow coffee or tea (without sugar or milk but with liquid non-caloric sweetener, if you wish) and mineral water. You can mix the mineral water with a total of 1 cup dry white wine for the two days. It is important that you rotate the foods over the course of the weekend.

Weight loss: Up to 4 pounds.

Buttermilk Diet

This gives dramatic results. You can drink 2 quarts buttermilk each day for two days; flavor it with fresh herbs or fresh fruit juices if you wish. Fruit juice may only be sweetened with liquid non-caloric sweetener.

Weight loss: 3 to 4 pounds.

Chicken Diet

This is the simplest diet there is. For breakfast have 2 slices crispbread, thinly spread with butter or margarine, and black coffee or tea. For lunch and dinner eat half a broiled chicken, skin removed. Accompany with a fresh salad; use a vinegar dressing without oil, but with plenty of herbs. Beverages allowed are coffee, tea, herb tea and mineral water.

Weight loss: 2 to 3 pounds.

Crispbread Diet

This diet is perfect for working people. During the day eat 2 slices crispbread three times a day, topping it with 2 ounces raw ground beef round (seasoned), 2 hard-cooked eggs, 1 ounce Edam cheese and as much tomato and cucumber as you want. If you prefer, sustitute a total of 6 ounces ground meat and omit egg and cheese. Between meals you can get another 4 slices melba toast. Drink plenty of liquids with this diet: 2 cups coffee with milk are permitted each day, and you can also have black coffee, tea, mineral water and skim milk.

Weight loss: Up to 4 pounds.

Egg Diet

Caution: Do not follow this diet if you have high blood cholesterol or any kidney problems. Each day, eat 2 freshly-cooked eggs for breakfast, 1 egg mid-morning and for lunch 2 eggs with a big portion of fresh salad, prepared without oil. In the afternoon eat 1 cooked egg. Supper is 2 eggs again, cooked without fat and served with steamed spinach (as much as you want). Drink plenty of mineral water, fruit tea or herb tea; coffee and black tea are also allowed.

Weight loss: 3 to 4 pounds.

Endive Diet

You can eat 3 pounds Belgian endive each day. For breakfast, add for each day a hard-cooked egg and 2 slices rye crispbread, with coffee or tea. For steamed endive, heat ¼ cup broth (made from bouillon cubes) in a skillet. Place 1 pound endive, halved lengthwise, into the broth cut side down. Cover and simmer 20 minutes, then season to taste with salt, nutmeg, curry or sweet paprika. For salad, chop 1 pound endive. Mix with sections from 1 medium orange. Mix a dressing of liquid non-caloric sweetener, a few drops oil, salt and pepper and add to endive; or

if you prefer, dress the salad with plain yogurt instead. You can drink mineral water, coffee or tea.

Weight loss: Up to 4 pounds.

Fruit Diet

Each day have 3 pounds of fruit of your choice. Eat as is, or prepare fruit salad with liquid non-caloric sweetener; up to half of the fruit can also be cooked. Through the day eat 3 slices crispbread or zwieback. Drink a little coffee or tea, mineral water or low-calorie lemonade, but have the beverages between rather than with meals.

Weight loss: Up to 4 pounds.

Grape Diet

Eat 4 pounds of grapes in two days. You can have small amounts of grape juice as well, but the whole fruit is more satisfying and the fiber in the skins prevents constipation.

Weight loss: 3 to 4 pounds.

Milk Diet

During the day have 1½ quarts whole milk, or 1 quart milk and 1 pound farmer cheese; mix cheese with water until creamy and season to taste with spices, liquid non-caloric sweetener and some instant coffee if you wish. Drink coffee or tea with this diet.

Weight loss: Up to 2 pounds.

Oatmeal Diet

Obviously, for oatmeal lovers. On the first day have five meals, each consisting of ½ cup freshly pressed, unsweetened fruit juice mixed with 2 tablespoons instant oatmeal and eaten at once. The diet for the second day is as follows: Breakfast: Mixture of ¼ cup instant or quick-cooking oatmeal, 1 medium orange, sectioned, and liquid non-caloric sweetener and lemon juice to taste. Mid-morning: 1 medium apple. Lunch: Mixture of ¼ cup instant or quick-cooking oatmeal, 1 medium apple, 1 small pear, sections of 1 small orange, lemon juice and liquid non-caloric sweetener. Afternoon: 1 medium orange. Supper: 1 cup fresh fruit juice with 3 tablespoons instant oatmeal. Drink mineral water, tea and coffee as desired.

Weight loss: Up to 4 pounds.

Potato Diet

Eat 2½ pounds of boiled potatoes divided over the entire day. For lunch and dinner prepare a sauce made of 4 ounces (½ cup) farmer cheese seasoned to taste with salt, pepper, curry powder, paprika and herbs and beaten with a little water until smooth. Drink coffee, tea, fruit or herb tea and mineral water.

Weight loss: 2 to 4 pounds.

Rice Diet

Each day cook 8 ounces (1¼ cups) brown or converted rice in unsalted boiling water. Cook 1 pound apples into a thick sauce and mix with rice; the mixture should be creamy, not very thick. Flavor with liquid non-caloric sweetener and cinnamon. Divide into small portions to be eaten during the day. For beverages, coffee, tea and mineral water are allowed, or 2 cups beer if you have no problems with fluid retention.

Weight loss: Up to 4 pounds.

Sauerkraut Diet

Breakfast: 2 slices crispbread and 1 cooked egg, with coffee or tea. Lunch: 2 cups (12 ounces) cooked sauerkraut with 1 frankfurter. Afternoon and supper: 1 cup (6 ounces) uncooked sauerkraut.

Weight loss: 2 to 4 pounds.

Vegetable Diet

This is one of the best short diets, since it is satisfying and healthy. Each day have a breakfast of 1 egg and 2 slices crispbread, spread thinly with butter or margarine. Drink coffee or tea. During the rest of the day have 3 pounds vegetables of your choice, divided to last all day long to keep your stomach from growling. Vegetables can be steamed in a little broth or made into salad; the salad can be dressed with plenty of plain yogurt, or with vinegar to which you can add a few drops of oil.

Weight loss: 4 pounds.

Please note: Do not follow any of these diets for more than two days, and leave at least a two-week interval between weekend diets. One more point: Eat lightly after your diet so that your stomach has a chance to adjust to normal intake.

Notes on Nutrition

All the recipes in this book are based on principles of modern nutrition. But here's additional information for those who want to reform their eating habits permanently.

The Basic Foods for Energy

The correctly balanced diet contains protein, fat and carbohydrate for growth and energy. Also vital are minerals, vitamins, fiber and water. These nutrients must be eaten in both correct amounts and the correct proportions. Each day's usual calorie intake should comprise 12 to 15 percent protein, 30 to 35 percent fat and 50 to 55 percent carbohydrate. In a reducing diet, calorie distribution shifts to a larger proportion of protein, which satisfies without the calories of fat: 25 percent protein, 2 ounces fat and 6 ounces carbohydrate daily for a diet providing 1500 calories.

Protein: Essential to Life

No one can live without protein: It is *the* most important nutrient. The body cells are made of protein, which in turn is composed of building blocks called amino acids. Twenty-five of these amino acids are essential to life; eight of them must be supplied by food as they are not synthesized by the body. The protein needed for each pound of body weight is:

Infants	1.1 g
Toddlers	1.0 g
Children and youths	.9 to .6 g
Adults	.5 g
Older adults	.6 g
Pregnant and nursing mothers	.6 to .7 g

These requirements vary according to individual circumstances. Athletes, for example, need more protein than inactive people. Those on reducing diets need more protein to feel satisfied.

Both plant and animal foods provide protein, but plant proteins are present in far smaller amounts and are incomplete. Nutrition experts recommend that ⅓ of our daily protein intake should come from animal sources and ⅔ from plant sources; animal protein contains the essential amino acids in the correct proportions, and having both in the same meal means the animal foods can complement the incomplete amino acids of the plant proteins. So, for example, the mixture of eggs and potatoes in one dish is ideal.

The Lower the Fat, the Higher the Protein

So that you will know what to eat when you are not following one of the recipes in this book, here is a short list of the most important low-fat protein sources.

The following are sources of animal protein:

Cottage, skim milk or farmer cheese
Plain yogurt
Skim milk or buttermilk
Varieties of cheese with 30% fat or lower
Lean meat such as beef filet, veal cutlet or leg, ground beef round
Variety meats
Game
Chicken and turkey (especially the breast, without skin)
Lean fish and seafood such as shrimp, shellfish, haddock, trout, cod and sole
Egg White

These are sources of plant protein:

Soybeans, soy flour, soy flakes and other low-fat soy products (soy provides some of the most valuable of all plant proteins)
Yeast, wheat kernels, nuts (sadly, the latter are high in calories but rich in unsaturated fatty acids)
Legumes, oat or wheat flakes and whole-grain breads, including whole-grain crispbreads

Usually the body uses protein chiefly for building and repairing cells, while the energy needed for physical activity is supplied by fat and carbohydrate. When fat and carbohydrate intake are restricted, however, protein is used for energy.

Fat Makes Fat

Because we no longer work as hard as we did 50 years ago, and so need less energy for muscular activity, we must reduce our fat consumption to keep from gaining weight.

Fats are not all the same. As most people know by now, the healthfulness of various fats depends on their content of saturated versus polyunsaturated fatty acids. Though both are found in animal as well as plant foods, animal fats are more saturated, while plant fats—for example, corn, soy and sunflower oils, and margarines made with them—contain higher proportions of the polyunsaturated fatty acids that the body needs each day. Linoleic acid, formerly called vitamin F, is the most important of the polyunsaturated fatty acids. Like the others, it helps maintain blood cholesterol and triglycerides at correct levels and even lowers them. Polyunsaturated fatty acids can also lessen the effects of heart and circulatory diseases. At least 35 percent of your daily fat intake should be of oils with a high proportion of polyunsturated fatty acids. They should not be heated at all if possible.

The Fatal Hidden Fats

A large part of our excess fat calories comes from hidden fats. Here are some of the worst culprits, the numbers representing the grams of fat per 100 g (3½ ounces):

	GRAMS
Bacon	89
Beef, ground	25
Beef, roast	19
Bologna	27
Chicken, fried	11
Duck	17
Fish sticks	8
Frankfurters	21
Goose	31
Ham, cooked	21
Ham, raw cured	33
Hamburger (average)	20
Lamb	32
Liver pate	29
Liverwurst	41
Pork, cooked	31
Pork sausage	32
Tongue	16
American Cheese	30
Swiss cheese	28
Ice cream	12
Whipped cream	30
Mayonnaise	80
Almonds	54

	GRAMS
Brazil nuts	67
Hazelnuts	62
Peanuts	47
Walnuts	63
French fries	13
Apple pie	11
Chocolate	33
Macaroons	24
Marzipan	18
Nougat	35
Piecrust	26
Puff pastry	38

Don't Forget Carbohydrates

Years ago "starches" were considered fattening, but nutritionists today are unanimous in their advice: Don't forget carbohydrates! Refined sugar—including brown sugar—is pure, concentrated calories. This is not true, however, of the complex carbohydrates in vegetables, fruit and grains. They are our basic energy source and these foods also provide essential vitamins, minerals and other trace elements.

Fiber Is Important

The importance of fruits and vegetables lies not only in their complex carbohydrates, but also in the non-digestible carbohydrates—or fiber—now known to be an absolute necessity. Sad to say, we eat too little fiber in the form of fruit, vegetables and grain products, and too many foods with a large proportion of refined carbohydrates and empty calories.

High-fiber foods help prevent intestinal malfunction. Nutritionists recommend the consumption of at least 25 g of fiber each day. Of the following foods, 100 g (3½ ounces) contain the indicated grams of fiber:

	GRAMS
Almonds	2.6
Apples (peeled)	9
Artichokes	1.5
Beans, dry	4
Brazil nuts	3
Cabbage	8
Carrots	6

	GRAMS
Corn	3
Crispbread	2
Hazelnuts	3.5
Lentils	4
Lettuce	12
Oats	13
Oranges (peeled)	3
Peanuts, roasted	2.7
Peas	2
Rice bran	13
Rye bread, whole-grain	1.6
Rye germ	3.7
Wheat bran	11
Wheat bread, whole-grain	1

All Our Vitamins

Everyone knows that vitamins are essential to health and that nearly all must be supplied in the food we eat. Vitamin deficiency leads to multiple symptoms: decreased performance, fatigue, chills, skin diseases and, in extreme cases, death. If you decrease your food consumption for a long period of time be sure to take a vitamin supplement daily.

Here is an outline of what the various vitamins do and in which foods they are most plentiful:

Fat-Soluble Vitamins

The body stores fat-soluble vitamins, so, while they are essential to health, they need not be consumed every single day.

- Vitamin A—daily requirement about 2500 IU. Found in variety meats, milk products such as butter and cheese, and eggs; also, in the form of carotene, in fruits and vegetables. Vitamin A is important for growth of bones and teeth, and for good eyesight.
- Vitamin D—daily requirement 400 IU. Found in fortified milk products, eggs, liver, mushrooms. Required for proper absorption of calcium and phosphorus; maintains strong bones and teeth, normal heart action and blood clotting.
- Vitamin E—daily requirement about 30 IU. Found in plant oils, leafy green vegetables, meat, seeds, wheat germ. Regulates the utilization of water and fat. Protects heart, blood vessels, muscles and reproductive system. As an anticoagulant, helps prevent stroke.

Water-Soluble Vitamins

When water-soluble vitamins are taken in excessive amounts, whatever goes unused is eliminated in the urine.

- Thiamin (Vitamin B_1)—daily requirement 1 to 2 mg. Found in liver, whole grain products, eggs, potatoes, dry beans, dark green vegetables, nuts, yeast, poultry and pork. Important to the proper utilization of carbohydrates.
- Riboflavin (Vitamin B_2)—daily requirement 1 to 2 mg. Found in milk (1 quart provides a whole day's amount), yeast, egg yolk, organ meats, dry beans, whole grain products, leafy green vegetables. Important to the proper utilization of protein, fat and carbohydrates.
- Niacin (Vitamin B_3)—daily requirement 20 mg. Found in liver, meat, poultry, legumes. Needed to release energy from carbohydrates, proteins and fats.
- Vitamin B_6—daily requirement about 2.5 mg. Found in yeast, legumes, leafy green vegetables, muscle meat, liver, egg yolks, milk, fish, avocado, potatoes and whole grain products. Important to proper digestion, especially that of protein, and to proper functioning of the central nervous system.
- Vitamin B_{12}—daily requirement 3 to 10 micrograms. Found in organ meats, seafood and eggs. Vitamin B_{12} is important to red blood cell formation and the utilization of food for this purpose, as well as for healthy nervous tissue.
    A well-balanced, varied diet contains the amounts needed of the entire vitamin B group.
- Vitamin C—daily requirement 60 mg. Found in fruits (especially citrus), raw vegetables and liver. Vitamin C protects against infection and aids in cell building and hormone production. Vitamin C should be increased during strenuous dieting. Smokers should also take Vitamin C supplements.

Minerals: Small Amounts, but All-Important

Minerals are divided into two groups: those of which we need larger amounts (over 100 mg) daily, and trace elements, needed only in tiny fractions of a gram. To the first group belong calcium, potassium, magnesium, sodium and phosphorus. Trace elements include iron, zinc, manganese, iodine and a number of others.

- Calcium—daily requirement 800 mg. Present (in milligram amounts) in almost all foods, but the largest amount is to be found in milk and milk products, shellfish, eggs, sardines, salmon, broccoli, okra and dry beans. Essential for healthy teeth and bones, transmission of nerve impulses and regulation of contractions (including muscle heartbeat).
- Potassium—daily requirement about 2 g. Found in fruits and vegetables. Potassium regulates the fluid content and waste elimination of the body's cells.
- Magnesium—daily requirement 350 mg. Found in green vegetables, whole grains, legumes, nuts, seeds and poultry. Important for proper digestion of all food: carbohydrates, protein and fats.
- Sodium—daily requirement 2 to 3 g. Present in many foods, especially animal products; a balanced diet provides plenty of sodium. It is the principal component of table salt, or sodium chloride. The use of salt should be kept as low as possible, since too much salt retains fluids in the body and raises blood pressure. Sodium is used in the digestive tract for splitting starch molecules and utilizing protein.
- Phosphorus—daily requirement 800 mg. Found in milk, meat, fish, poultry, eggs, whole grains, nuts, legumes. Necessary for body's utilization of calcium and for absorption of other nutrients.

Trace Elements

- Iron—daily requirement about 15 mg. Present in trace amounts in all kinds of meat and meat products, especially liver, but also in whole-grain wheat products, oysters, clams, dry beans. The body needs iron for oxygen transfer in the blood, and a high iron intake is important to prevent anemia during pregnancy.

Generally speaking, .1 percent of our body is composed of trace elements. In addition to iron are iodine, selenium, manganese, copper, zinc, chromium, fluorine and molybdenum. A varied, well balanced diet provides all of these trace minerals.

Brief Calorie Chart

Understandably, the following chart is not complete, but will give you an idea of the calorie content of the most important foods. Should you need one, extensive calorie charts are widely available.

These calorie counts are based on a 3½-ounce edible portion of food, weighed after removing bones, skin and waste.

	CALORIES
Ale	42
Almonds	598
Anchovies	164
Angel food cake	269
Apples, unpeeled	60
Apple butter	186
Apple jelly	260
Apple juice	47
Applesauce	79
Apricots	54
Apricots, canned in heavy syrup	86
Apricot jam	257
Apricot nectar	57
Artichoke	40
Asparagus	20
Avocado	170
Bacon	611
Bacon, Canadian	277
Bamboo shoots	27
Bananas	85
Barley	349
Bass, freshwater	105
Beans, baked	125
Beans, green	25
Beans, lima	111
Beans, wax	22

	CALORIES
Beans, white	352
Beansprouts, mung	35
Beef, corned	372
Beef, dried, chipped	203
Beef, filet	126
Beef, flank steak	190
Beef, ground	126
Beef, round	261
Beets	32
Beet greens	18
Blackberries	58
Blood sausage	425
Blueberries	62
Bluefish	159
Bologna	304
Bouillon, made from cubes	7
Brandy	215
Bratwurst, veal	343
Brazil nuts	654
Bread, Boston brown	211
Bread, cracked wheat	263
Bread, French	280
Bread, pumpernickel	246
Bread, raisin	262
Bread, rye	243
Bread, white	270
Bread, wholewheat	242
Breadcrumbs, dry	382
Broccoli	26
Brussels sprouts	36
Bulgur	356
Butter	716
Butter, whipped	393

	CALORIES		CALORIES
Buttermilk	36	Cranberry sauce	146
Cabbage, green	20	Cream, whipping	352
Cabbage, Chinese	14	Cucumbers	14
Cantaloupe	30	Currants, dried	325
Caramels	399	Dates	274
Carrots	42	Duck	165
Casaba melon	30	Eel, smoked	330
Cashews	561	Eggs	163
Catfish	103	Eggplant	20
Catsup	106	Elderberries	72
Cauliflower	22	Endive, Belgian	15
Caviar	262	Escarole	20
Celery	17	Farina, cooked	42
Celery root	40	Fennel	28
Cervelat, soft	307	Figs	80
Chard	18	Figs, dried	274
Chayote	28	Fish sticks	176
Cheese, American	370	Flounder	83
Cheese, bleu	368	Flour	368
Cheese, Brie	368	Frankfurters	304
Cheese, Camembert	299	Frogs' legs	73
Cheese, Cheddar	398	Fruitcake	155
Cheese, cottage, creamed	106	Gin	231
Cheese, cottage, uncreamed	86	Ginger ale	31
Cheese, cream	374	Ginger, candied	340
Cheese, Parmesan	393	Gingerbread	317
Cheese, Swiss	370	Goose	441
Cherries, Bing	70	Gooseberries	39
Cherries, maraschino	116	Grapefruit	41
Cherries, sour	58	Grapefruit juice	39
Chestnuts	194	Grapes	67
Chicken broiled	136	Grape juice	66
Chicken roll	243	Guavas	62
Chickpeas, dry	360	Gumdrops	347
Chocolate, milk	520	Half and half	134
Chocolate, semisweet	507	Halibut	171
Clams	80	Ham, canned	193
Coconut, fresh	346	Ham, country-style	389
Coconut, dried sweetened	548	Ham, deviled	351
Cod	170	Hazelnuts	634
Cola	39	Headcheese	268
Coleslaw	144	Hearts of palm, canned	40
Collards	32	Herring, kippered	211
Corn	83	Herring, pickled	223
Cornbread	224	Honey	304
Cornstarch	360	Honeydew melon	30
Crabmeat	93	Horseradish, prepared	38
Crackers, animal	429	Ice cream	200
Crackers, cheese	479	Ice milk	152
Crackers, graham	384	Jelly beans	367
Crackers, soda	439	Kale	28
Cranberries	46	Knackwurst	278

	CALORIES		CALORIES
Kohlrabi	24	Oranges	49
Kumquats	65	Orange juice	45
Ladyfingers	360	Oysters, canned	76
Lamb, leg	279	Pancakes	231
Lamb, shoulder	338	Papayas	39
Lard	902	Parsley	44
Leeks	38	Parsnips	66
Lemons	27	Peaches	38
Lemonade	44	Peaches, canned in heavy syrup	78
Lentils, cooked	106	Peaches, dried	262
Lettuce, iceberg	13	Peach nectar	48
Lettuce, leaf	18	Peanuts	585
Limes	28	Peanut brittle	421
Limeade	41	Peanut butter	589
Liver, beef	229	Pears, unpeeled	61
Liver, calves'	261	Pears, canned in heavy syrup	76
Liverwurst	307	Pears, dried	268
Lobster	95	Pear nectar	52
Macadamia nuts	691	Peas, blackeye	76
Macaroni, cooked	129	Peas, Chinese	43
Mackerel	236	Peas, green	71
Mandarin oranges	48	Peas, split, cooked	115
Mangoes	66	Pecans	687
Maple syrup	252	Peppers, green	22
Margarine	720	Peppers, red	31
Marmalade	257	Perch	89
Marshmallows	319	Persimmons	127
Mayonnaise	718	Pickles, sour	10
Milk, condensed	321	Pickles, sweet	146
Milk, evaporated	137	Pie, apple	256
Milk, low fat	59	Pie, Boston cream	302
Milk, skimmed	36	Pie, cherry	261
Milk, whole	66	Pie, coconut custard	235
Mortadella	315	Pie, lemon meringue	255
Muffins, bran	261	Pie, mince	271
Muffins, corn	314	Pie, peach	255
Muffins, plain	294	Pie, pecan	418
Mushrooms	28	Pie, pumpkin	211
Mushrooms, canned	25	Pimientos, canned	27
Mussels	95	Pineapple	56
Mustard greens	23	Pineapple, canned in heavy syrup	74
Mustard, prepared, brown	91	Pineapple juice	55
Mustard, prepared, yellow	75	Pine nuts	552
Nectarines	64	Pistachios	594
Noodles, chow mein	489	Pizza	236
Noodles, cooked	125	Plums	75
Oatmeal, cooked	55	Plums, canned in heavy syrup	83
Octopus	73	Popcorn, popped	386
Oil	884	Popovers	224
Okra	29	Pork, cutlet	358
Olives, green, stuffed	116	Pork, fresh ham	374
Onions	38	Pork, loin	391

111

	CALORIES		CALORIES
Pork, picnic shoulder	374	Squash, summer	14
Pork, spareribs	440	Squash, winter	38
Potatoes, baked	93	Squid	84
Potatoes, boiled	70	Strawberries	37
Potatoes, French fried	274	Strawberries, in syrup	110
Potato chips	568	Strawberry jam	260
Pretzels	390	Sturgeon, smoked	149
Prunes	255	Sugar, brown	373
Prune juice	77	Sugar, fruit (fructose)	433
Puff pastry, frozen	410	Sugar, granulated	385
Pumpkin, canned	33	Sugar, powdered	385
Rabbit	216	Sunflower seed kernels	560
Radishes	17	Sweetbreads, veal	168
Raisins	289	Sweet potatoes	128
Raspberries	57	Swordfish	174
Raspberries, in syrup	111	Tangerines	46
Raspberry jam	271	Tapioca pudding	134
Rhubarb, cooked, sweetened	141	Tartar sauce	531
Rice, brown, cooked	119	Tilefish	138
Rice, white, cooked	109	Tomatoes	22
Root beer	41	Tomato juice	19
Rum	231	Tomato paste	82
Rutabagas	35	Tomato puree	39
Salami, cooked	311	Tongue, beef	255
Salami, dry	450	Trout	168
Salmon, canned	171	Tuna, canned in oil	197
Salmon, smoked	176	Tuna, canned in water	127
Sardines, canned	203	Turkey	190
Sauerkraut	18	Turnips	23
Sausage, breakfast	476	Turnip greens	20
Scallops	112	Veal, loin	234
Sesame seed	582	Veal, round	216
Shad	201	Vegetables, mixed	64
Shallots	72	Venison	126
Sherbet	134	Vienna sausage	240
Shrimp	91	Vodka	231
Snapper	93	Waffles	279
Sole	79	Walnuts	651
Soup, bean	67	Water chestnuts	79
Soup, beef noodle	28	Watercress	19
Soup, chicken noodle	26	Watermelon	26
Soup, onion	27	Wheat bran	213
Soup, split pea	59	Wheat germ	363
Soup, tomato	36	Whisky	249
Soup, vegetable	32	Whitefish	108
Soybeans, cooked	130	Wine, dessert	137
Soybean curd (tofu)	72	Wine, table	85
Soy flour	469	Yams	101
Soy sauce	68	Yellowtail	138
Spaghetti, cooked	129	Yogurt, part skim	50
Spinach	23	Zwieback	423

Staying Thin While Eating Out

What about those of us who must eat frequent restaurant meals? It is often impossible to avoid eating out, but there are lots of tricks as to what to eat and what to leave alone.

- Skip the previous meal and munch on raw vegetables or a salad instead. Raw vegetables take time to digest, so your stomach will have something to work on until the next meal. Before going out, drink a glass of vegetable juice. This will curtail your appetite and supply you with valuable vitamins and minerals.
- If you are offered a drink before the meal, accept it without protest and sip it, but don't finish it unless your calorie count permits. You can place the glass aside unnoticed.
- If you are lucky, the menu will include roast beef, steak, poultry or game—all lean foods from which you can take a moderate portion. Leave the gourmet concoctions for others to eat.
- If interesting conversation flows your companions won't notice what you eat, and no one will be tempted to urge you to have more.
- One or two glasses of red or white wine will not drastically throw off your calorie count. But be careful: alcohol increases your appetite, while your food intake should be a little smaller to compensate. It's even better, naturally, to stay away from alcohol.
- When *kaffeeklatscher* friends offer you cake, take the smallest and least-frosted piece. And only one: surely it will have enough calories.
- On the day before and the day after a party, eat mini portions or use one of the weekend diets. This way you'll be able to cheat a little at the party.

Here is a list of what to eat in restaurants:

1. Meat: All kinds of filets, steak tartare, veal, variety meats, lean lamb, poultry, game—broiled and without sauce.
2. Milk products: Farmer cheese, yogurt, skim milk, cheeses with maximum 30% fat such as Edam, Camembert, Tilsiter, cottage cheese and hard cheeses. Only a few spoonfuls of high-fat milk dishes and ice cream.
3. Vegetables: All sorts, without sauce but steamed with a little butter. Also, vegetable soup with lean meat. You have to be sparing only with potatoes: Three small boiled potatoes or one portion mashed fit into your calorie count.
4. Fish: Most varieties, best poached, broiled or steamed in their own juices. *Not* breaded or fried in butter.
5. Baked Foods/Sweets/nuts: Whole-grain and other bread (two slices), a little salt stick, a few nuts, a tiny piece of cake or a few cookies. Gelatin dishes are usually moderate in calories; also, low-fat ice cream, ice milk or sherbet.

Buying the Right Foods

Whoever wishes to eat healthful foods must be knowledgeable about how to purchase them. Here are a few pointers:

- Try to select whole grain products instead of those made with white flour. Buy converted rice or brown rice products, not regular hulled white rice.
- Vegetables (including potatoes) and fruits contain good complex carbohydrates with vitamins, minerals and trace elements. They should be reduced as little as possible during your diet.
- Meat, poultry and fish, the leaner the better, are the most important sources of protein. Variety meats, in particular, are also rich in minerals and vitamins.
- Milk products of every form contain vitamins and minerals. Just stay away from high-fat choices.

- Select natural oils and margarine made from them. Both should have a high proportion of poly-unsaturated fatty acids.
- Wheat germ, brewer's yeast and soy flakes (as well as other soy products) should be put at the top of your shopping list. All three can be sprinkled on food to add taste and nutrients, each contributing about 40 calories per tablespoon. Vitamin-rich vegetable juices are also a boon for nutrition-conscious dieters.
- Natural oils are affected by light and temperature. Buy cooking or salad oil in small amounts; if you must buy more, keep it in a cool, dark place or in the refrigerator.
- Almost all packaged, perishable foods are marked with pull dates. Watch for them, as these dates are critical for the freshness and wholesomeness of the product.

Tips for Slimming and Staying Slim

These are the basic rules for the figure-conscious. If you heed them, you will be slim now and forever.

- Always have five meals a day, but don't go over your calorie requirement.
- Eat small portions on small plates to make servings seem larger.
- Eat slowly and intelligently. Chew carefully and pause between bites. Be conscious of tasting every mouthful.
- Use suger sparingly and replace it with non-caloric sweeteners when feasible.
- Use less fat wherever possible. Purchase lean foods and use little or no fat for cooking; food contains enough hidden fat. Make it a habit to remove all visible fat from meat, sausage and ham. One gram of fat has 9.3 calories; 10 grams, 93. You should remember these numbers.
- Always aim for a high-protein diet, since protein satisfies. Lean animal foods such as meat, fish, poultry, game, low-fat cheeses and milk products have the largest proportion of protein.
- Drastically reduce the amount of sweets and pastries you eat.
- Everything for nibbling should be removed from sight so you are not tempted. Family and friends should be asked to understand and cooperate.
- Move, play sports, dance. Use the steps instead of the elevator and keep the car in the garage more often. This not only speeds your effort to lose pounds, but also improves your circulation, muscle tone and general well-being.
- Omit high-calorie beverages such as sweetened fruit drinks, soda and, above all, alcohol.

- Keep yourself occupied with reading or a hobby to keep from thinking about food. Boredom is the worst enemy of people who are trying to lose weight.
- Note the calorie counts of the most important foods so that you will shop more intelligently.
- Never go marketing when you are hungry. This leads to shopping mistakes.
- Cook and sauté in nonstick pans, or broil whenever possible. In this way fat is removed from food, not added to it.
- Even the smallest amount of leftovers has calories. Do not make yourself the family garbage pail. Do not finish everything "so it doesn't go to waste." Your health and well-being are more important.
- And don't ever say "A few calories won't hurt me." A few too many calories every day can, in a few weeks, produce fat deposits.
- No matter how delicious it is, eat just half the portion. This applies especially to people who frequently eat away from home.
- Don't let anyone talk you into eating—certainly not with silly rationalizations like "this little piece won't hurt." You know better how many extra calories a small piece of cake has.
- Control your weight constantly, not just when coat or pants no longer fit. Just a small increase on the scale should give you the impetus to do something.
- Make it a habit not to have supper any later than 7 p.m.
- Eat a varied, balanced diet until you reach your ideal weight. And, it is to be hoped, forever.

The following are conversion tables and other information applicable to those converting the recipes in this book for use in other English-speaking countries. The cup and spoon measures given in this book are U.S. Customary; use these tables when working with British Imperial or Metric kitchen utensils.

Metric—Imperial Conversion Table

Liquid Measures

The old Imperial pint is larger than the U.S. pint; therefore note the following when measuring the liquid ingredients.

U.S.	IMPERIAL
1 cup = 8 fluid ounces	1 cup = 10 fluid ounces
½ cup = 4 fluid ounces	½ cup = 5 fluid ounces
1 tablespoon = ½ fluid ounce	1 tablespoon = 1 fluid ounce

U.S. MEASURE	METRIC	IMPERIAL*	
1 quart	946 mL	1½ +	pints
1 pint	473 mL	¾ +	pint
1 cup	236 mL	− ½	pint
1 tablespoon	15 mL	− 1	tablespoon
1 teaspoon	5 mL	− 1	teaspoon

Oven Temperatures

Gas Mark	¼	2	4	6	8
Fahrenheit	225	300	350	400	450
Celsius	110	150	180	200	230

*Note that exact quantities cannot always be given. Differences are more crucial when dealing with larger quantities. For teaspoon and tablespoon measures, simply use scant quantities, or for more accurate conversions rely upon metric measures.

Weight and Volume Measures

U.S. cooking procedures usually measure certain items by volume, although in the Metric or Imperial systems they are measured by weight. Here are some approximate equivalents for basic items.*

	U.S. CUSTOMARY	METRIC	IMPERIAL
Apples (peeled and sliced)	4 cups	450 g	1 pound
Beans, dried (raw)	2½ cups	450 g	1 pound
Butter	1 cup	225 g	8 ounces
	½ cup	115 g	4 ounces
	¼ cup	60 g	2 ounces
	1 tablespoon	15 g	½ ounce
Cheese (grated)	½ cup	60 g	2 ounces
Cornstarch	1 teaspoon	10 g	⅓ ounce
Cream of Tartar	1 teaspoon	3–4 g	⅛ ounce
Flour, all-purpose	1 cup	140 g	5 ounces
(sifted)	½ cup	70 g	2½ ounces
	¼ cup	35 g	1¼ ounces
Herbs, fresh	¼ cup chopped	7 g	¼ ounce
	2 tablespoons chopped	7 g	¼ ounce
Mushrooms, fresh (chopped)	4 cups	300 g	10 ounces
Nut meats	1 cup	115 g	4 ounces
Peas, fresh (shelled)	1 cup	115 g	4 ounces
Potatoes (mashed)	2 cups	450 g	1 pound
Raisins (or Sultanas)	¾ cup	125 g	4½ ounces
Rice	1 cup (raw)	225 g	8 ounces
	3 cups (cooked)	225 g	8 ounces
Spinach, fresh (cooked)	1 cup	285 g	10 ounces
Sugar:	1 cup	190 g	6½ ounces
granulated/brown	½ cup	85 g	3 ounces
	¼ cup	40 g	1¾ ounces
	1 tablespoon	5 g	½ ounce
confectioners'	1 cup	80 g	5 ounces
	½ cup	40 g	3 ounces
	¼ cup	20 g	1 + ounce
	1 tablespoon	5 g	½ ounce
Tomatoes, fresh (peeled, seeded, juiced)	1½ cups	450 g	1 pound
Zucchini	3½ cups (sliced)	450 g	1 pound
	2 cups (grated)	300 g	5 ounces

117

*So as to avoid awkward measurements, some conversions are not exact.

Index

119